It's another Quality Book from CGP

This book is for anyone doing GCSE Mathematics at Higher Level.

It contains lots of tricky questions designed
to make you sweat — because that's the only
way you'll get any better.

What CGP is all about

Our sole aim here at CGP is to produce the highest quality
books — carefully written, immaculately presented and
dangerously close to being funny.

Then we work our socks off to get them out to you
— at the cheapest possible prices.

Contents

Published by Coordination Group Publications Ltd.

Contributors:

Cath Brown, Peter Clegg, Margaret Darlington, Michael Davidson, Christine Graham, Tony Herbert, Sharon Keeley, Alan Mason, Andy Park, Julie Schofield, Alice Shepperson, Emma Singleton.

ISBN: 1-84146-311-6

Groovy website: www.cgpbooks.co.uk

With thanks to Vicky Daniel and Glenn Rogers for the proofreading.
Jolly bits of clipart from CorelDRAW
Printed by Elanders Hindson, Newcastle upon Tyne

Types of Number

1 From the following list of numbers, find an example of each type of number below:

$$7 \quad 9 \quad 10 \quad 8 \quad 20$$

(a) A square number: ....

(b) A triangle number: ....

(c) A cube number: ....

(d) A prime number: ....

2 This question is about two special kinds of number.

(a) Find the sum of the first five square numbers. ....

....

(b) Find the product of the first five triangle numbers. ....

....

3 Place the following in order of size, starting with the smallest:

$$6^2 \quad 3^4 \quad 2^5 \quad 4^2 \quad 5^3$$

....

....

4  Which of the following numbers is prime?

$$2^3 \quad 15 \quad 29 \quad 51 \quad 3^2$$

....

5 Work out $2^3 \times 4^2$.

....

6 Find the value of x in each of the following:

(a) $2^x = 64$ ....

(b) $5^x = 125$ ....

(c) $3^x = 243$ ....

7 Circle TRUE or FALSE for each of the following statements:

(a) $3^2 = 2^3$ TRUE   FALSE   (b) $3^2 + 4^2 = 5^2$ TRUE   FALSE

Prime Numbers

1 List all the prime numbers between 40 and 60.

....

....

2 State all the prime numbers in the list below:

73   27   61   25   1   81

....

....

3 Find the product of the first five prime numbers.

....

....

4 Decide whether each of the following numbers is prime:

(a) 143 ....

....

(b) 257 ....

....

(c) 379 ....

....

5 If a and b are prime numbers, give an example to show that each of the following statements is **false**:

(a) $a + b$ is always even. ....

....

(b) $a \times b$ is always odd. ....

....

(c) $a^2 + b^2$ is always even. ....

....

Multiples, Factors and Prime Factors

1 From the numbers on the right, write down: **24   16   9   7   30**

   (a) a multiple of 5 ....

   (b) a factor of 36 ....

   (c) a multiple of both 6 and 8 ....

2 This question is about multiples and factors.

   (a) Write down the multiples of 6 between 40 and 50. ....

   (b) Write down all the factors of 60. ....

....

3 Any positive whole number can be expressed as the product of its prime factors.

   (a) Express 30 as a product of its prime factors. ....

....

   (b) Express 36 as a product of its prime factors. ....

....

   (c) Hence find the lowest common multiple (LCM) of 30 and 36. ....

....

4 The highest common factor (HCF) of two numbers is the largest number that divides into them both.

   (a) Express 48 as a product of its prime factors. ....

....

   (b) Express 108 as a product of its prime factors. ....

....

   (c) Hence find the HCF of 48 and 108. ....

5 a and b are prime numbers.

   Find a and b if $a^4 \times b = 80$. ....

....

Section One

Fractions

1 Work out the following:

(a) $\frac{1}{5}$ of £75.80 ....

(b) $\frac{3}{8}$ of 60.8 m ....

2 Place the following quantities a, b and c in order of size, smallest first:

$a = \frac{2}{3}$ of 120 $b = \frac{3}{4}$ of 80 $c = \frac{3}{5}$ of 70

....

....

3 Work out the following, giving your answers in their simplest form:

(a) $\frac{2}{3} \times \frac{9}{10}$ ....

(b) $3\frac{1}{7} \times 1\frac{1}{7}$ ....

4 Give your answers to the following in their simplest form:

(a) $\frac{3}{8} \div \frac{9}{10}$ ....

(b) $3\frac{1}{2} \div 1\frac{3}{4}$ ....

5 Find the area of a rectangle measuring $3\frac{4}{7}$ m by $1\frac{2}{5}$ m.

....

....

6 A fishing rod is $2\frac{1}{4}$ metres long.
How many equal sections of length $\frac{3}{8}$ metre can it be folded into?

....

....

7 If $a = \frac{3}{4}$ and $b = 2\frac{1}{2}$, find the value of $\frac{1}{a} + \frac{1}{b}$.

....

....

Fractions

1   Rewrite these fractions in order of size, smallest first:

$$\frac{7}{8} \qquad \frac{5}{6} \qquad \frac{3}{4} \qquad \frac{2}{3}$$

....

2   Find the values of a, b, c and d in the equations below:

$$\frac{a}{100} = \frac{12}{b} = \frac{c}{20} = \frac{45}{d} = \frac{3}{4}$$
$a = $ .... $b = $ .... $c = $ .... $d = $ ....

3 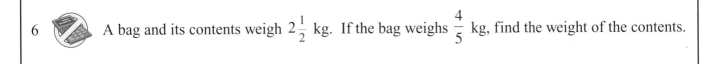 If $a = 3\frac{1}{2}$ and $b = 2\frac{3}{5}$, work out:

(a) $a + b$ ....

(b) $a - b$ ....

4 Amy walked $\frac{2}{3}$ km to the bus stop. She then travelled $3\frac{2}{5}$ km by bus.
What was the total length of her journey?

....

5 A rectangular field measures $1\frac{3}{4}$ km by $\frac{7}{8}$ km. What is the perimeter of the field?

....

6 A bag and its contents weigh $2\frac{1}{2}$ kg. If the bag weighs $\frac{4}{5}$ kg, find the weight of the contents.

....

7 Convert these mixed fractions into 'top-heavy' fractions:

(a) $3\frac{1}{8}$ .... (b) $2\frac{5}{6}$ ....

(c) $1\frac{15}{16}$ ....

8 Convert these 'top-heavy' fractions into mixed fractions:

(a) $\frac{17}{4}$ .... (b) $\frac{41}{7}$ .... (c) $\frac{35}{3}$ ....

Percentages

1   Work out:

(a) 30% of £80 ....

(b) 15% of 600 m ....

2   A computer costs £900 plus VAT, where VAT is charged at 17½%.
    What is the total cost of the computer?

    ....

3   In a school 57 pupils out of 128 in Year 9 reach level 5 in their Science examination.
    Express this amount of pupils as a percentage.

    ....

4   After an 8% pay rise Mr Brown's salary was £15,500.
    What was his salary before the increase?

    ....

    ....

5   This is a question about percentage loss and percentage gain.

(a) Mr Jones buys a house for £80,000 and later sells it for £95,000.
     Calculate his percentage profit.

     ....

(b) Mrs Evans buys a car for £17,000 and later sells it for £14,500.
     Calculate her percentage loss.

     ....

Rational and Irrational Numbers

1   Circle the rational numbers below:

$$-7 \qquad \sqrt{4} \qquad \pi \qquad 6.25 \qquad \sqrt{72} \qquad 5^{-1} \qquad \sqrt{64}$$

2   Pick any two numbers and you can always find a rational number and an irrational number between them.

  (a) Write down a rational number between 5 and 7. ....

  (b) Write down an irrational number between 5 and 7. ....

  (c) Write down a rational number between $\sqrt{5}$ and $\sqrt{7}$. ....

3   Rational numbers can always be expressed as fractions.

  (a) If p is a non-zero rational number, explain why $1/p$ must also be rational.

....

  (b) Write down two different irrational numbers p and q such that $\dfrac{p}{q}$ is a rational number.

....

4   If $x = \sqrt{2}$ and $y = 2\sqrt{2}$, state whether the following are rational or irrational:

  (a) xy ....

  (b) $x \div y$ ....

....

  (c) $x + y$ ....

....

5   If $p = 3 + \sqrt{2}$ and $q = 3 - \sqrt{2}$, work out each of the following and state whether your answers are rational or irrational:

  (a) $p + q$ ....

  (b) $p \times q$ ....

....

  (c) p^2 ....

....

Recurring Decimals and Surds

1 Write in the form $\frac{a}{b}$:

(a) $0.\dot{7}$ ....

(b) $0.\dot{2}\dot{6}$ ....

(c) $0.\dot{7}2\dot{9}$ ....

2 Circle TRUE or FALSE for each of the following statements:

(a) $\sqrt{32} = 4\sqrt{2}$ TRUE   FALSE   (b) $\sqrt{3}\sqrt{2} = \sqrt{6}$ TRUE   FALSE

(c) $\sqrt{4} + \sqrt{4} = \sqrt{8}$ TRUE   FALSE   (d) $(\sqrt{5})^2 = 5$ TRUE   FALSE

(e) $\frac{3}{\sqrt{3}} = \sqrt{3}$ TRUE   FALSE

3 Simplify the following as much as possible:

(a) $\sqrt{2} \times \sqrt{8}$ ....   (b) $\sqrt{48}$ ....

(c) $\sqrt{100}$ ....   (d) $5\sqrt{125}$ ....

(e) $\sqrt{27} + \sqrt{18}$ ....

4 Rationalising a denominator means making sure that there are no irrational numbers on the bottom line of a fraction.

(a) Simplify the following, making sure that the denominator is rational.

$\frac{2}{\sqrt{3}} \times \frac{3}{\sqrt{3}}$ ....

(b) Rationalise the denominator in these fractions:

(i) $\frac{3}{\sqrt{5}}$ ....

(ii) $\frac{5}{\sqrt{3}}$ ....

(iii) $\frac{7}{\sqrt{12}}$ ....

5 Answer these questions involving irrational products:

(a) Expand and simplify $(2 + \sqrt{3})(2 - \sqrt{3})$.

....

(b) Write $(2 + \sqrt{3})(5 - \sqrt{3})$ in the form $a + b\sqrt{3}$, where a and b are integers.

....

Finding the nth Term

1 A sequence of numbers is shown below.

4, 9, 14, 19,...

(a) Find the nth term. ....

(b) What is the 20th term? ....

(c) Which term has the value 209? ....

2 This question is also about sequences.

(a) Write down the next two terms in the sequence 3, 7, 11, 15,... ....

(b) Find the nth term of the sequence. ....

(c) Show that 502 cannot be a term in this sequence. ....

(d) Calculate the number of terms in the sequence 3, 7, 11, 15,…, 199. ....

....

3 Not all sequences increase by the same amount each time.

(a) Write down the next two terms in the sequence 3, 8, 15, 24,… ....

(b) Find the nth term of the sequence. ....

....

(c) What is the 30th term of the sequence? ....

4 The positive integers can be arranged as shown opposite:

The sequence of numbers 1, 3, 6, 10, 15,…
is formed by the last number in each row.

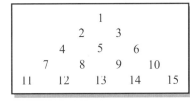

(a) What is the name of this sequence of numbers? ....

(b) Write down the next 3 numbers in the sequence. ....

(c) Find the nth term of this sequence. ....

....

(d) What is the 20th number in the sequence? ....

(e) Which term in the sequence has the value 820? ....

....

Conversion Factors, Metric and Imperial Units

1   Put these lengths in order of size, smallest first:

600 cm   2 yards   8 feet   3.6 m   70 inches

....

2   Circle TRUE or FALSE for each of the following statements:

(a) 5 kg < 10 lbs   TRUE   FALSE

(b) 8 litres > 2 gallons   TRUE   FALSE

(c) 6.5 inches is approximately equal to 16.25 cm   TRUE   FALSE

(d) 500 g < 1 lb   TRUE   FALSE

3   Mr Birchall travelled from London to Glasgow. He measured his journey as 400 miles.
    What is this distance in kilometres?

....

4   The petrol tank of Mrs Pardoe's car holds 20 gallons. How many litres is this?

....

5   A horse averaged a speed of 20 km per hour in a race. What is this speed in:

(a) metres per second?

....

(b) miles per hour?

....

6   The exchange rate is given as £1 = 1.65 US dollars.

(a) Change £300 to US dollars.   ....

(b) Convert 80 US dollars to pounds. ....

7   A map is drawn to a scale of 2 cm to 1 km.

(a) Work out the real length of a field which measures 5.6 cm on the map.

....

(b) The distance between two towns is 7.5 km. What is this distance on the map?

....

Accuracy and Estimating

1 Decide the appropriate accuracy for each of these measurements in the situation described, and round them off accordingly:

(a) A golfer trying to decide how high a tree is.

The exact height of the tree is 48.75 m. ....

(b) The club doctor wanting to know the weight of a footballer.

The footballer's exact weight is 78.2543 kg. ....

(c) A businessman wanting to know his average speed for a motorway journey.

His exact average speed was 76.593 mph. ....

2 Place these numbers in order of size, smallest first:

$$\sqrt{79} \qquad 8.5 \qquad \sqrt{60} \qquad 7.5 \qquad \sqrt{50}$$

....

3 Estimate each of the following to 1 decimal place:

(a) $\sqrt{23}$ .... (b) $\sqrt{38}$ ....

(c) $\sqrt{95}$ ....

4 Estimate the value of $\dfrac{523+694}{17.9+2.13}$, showing all your working.

....

....

5 The formula for the total surface area of a closed cylinder is $A = 2\pi r^2 + 2\pi rh$.
Estimate the surface area of a cylinder of base radius 1.89 cm and height 5.92 cm.

....

....

6 Estimate the size of these everyday objects:

(a) the volume of a family saloon car (in m^3) ....

....

(b) the area of the palm of your hand (in cm^2) ....

....

Rounding Off

1. The height of a plant is 18 cm, to the nearest cm.
What is the least possible total height of 7 such plants?

....

2. Bags of sand weigh 32 kg, to the nearest kg. What is the maximum weight of 8 bags of sand?

....

3. The time to run 100 m was recorded as 12.5 s, to the nearest 0.1 s.
State the upper and lower bounds of this time.

....

4. If $a = 2.8$ and $b = 3.6$ (both correct to 1 decimal place), find:

   (a) The maximum possible value of $a + b$ ....

   ....

   (b) The minimum possible value of $b - a$ ....

   ....

   (c) The maximum possible value of ab ....

   ....

   (d) The minimum possible value of $\dfrac{a}{b}$ ....

   ....

5. The sides of a triangle are given as 6 cm, 7 cm and 8 cm, correct to the nearest cm.

   (a) Work out the minimum possible perimeter of the triangle.

   ....

   (b) Work out the maximum percentage error in the perimeter if the rounded values
   are used to calculate it.

   ....

   ....

   ....

Numbers Mini-Exam (1)

1 Answer these questions without using a calculator:

(a) Work out $\frac{3}{5}$ of 16. ....

(b) Write down the value of $\sqrt{25} + 8^{\frac{2}{3}}$. ....

(c) Write down the value of $8^0 + 0.3^2$. ....

(d) Find an approximate value of $\frac{4.75}{18.4 + 1.9}$. ....

2 $n = 0.2\dot{7}\dot{8}$

(a) Write down the value of $1000n$. ....

(b) Hence express n as a fraction in its simplest form. ....

....

3 Numbers like $\sqrt{2}$ and $\sqrt{3}$ are irrational: they can't be expressed exactly as fractions.

(a) What is the area of a rectangle of side lengths $(5 + \sqrt{2})$ and $(3 - \sqrt{2})$?
Give your answer in the form $a + b\sqrt{2}$. ....

....

(b) If p is an irrational number, is $\frac{1 - p}{1 - p^2}$ rational or irrational?
Explain your answer. ....

....

4  Last year Amy was 80 cm tall and weighed 25 kg.

(a) She is now 5% taller. Calculate her height now.

....

(b) Amy weighs 30 kg now. Calculate her percentage increase in weight.

....

5 This is a question about sequences.

(a) Write down the first three terms of the sequence whose nth term is given by $\frac{5n}{n + 4}$.

....

(b) Which term of the sequence has a value of 4? ....

Numbers Mini-Exam (1)

6 From the list on th right, write down any: √25   61   9   15   2³   ³√8

   (a) prime numbers ....

   (b) multiples of 3 ....

   (c) triangle numbers ....

   (d) square numbers ....

   (e) factors of 30 ....

7 Here, HCF stands for highest common factor, and LCM stands for lowest common multiple.

   (a) Express 48 as a product of its prime factors. ....

   (b) Express 72 as a product of its prime factors. ....

   (c) Work out the HCF of 48 and 72. ....

   (d) Work out the LCM of 48 and 72. ....

8 A garden has an area of 500 m², of which 60% is lawn. One quarter of the rest is patio. What is the area of the patio?

....

....

9 Estimate the value of x to 1 decimal place:

   (a) $x^2 = 66$ ....

   (b) $2x^2 = 64$ ....

   (c) $x^3 = 70$ ....

10 A restaurant orders 40 litres of milk. 75 pints are delivered instead. Does the restaurant have enough milk? Show your working.

....

11 For each of the following, write down the value of x:

   (a) $x^3 = 216$ ....

   (b) $2^x = 64$ ....

   (c) $5^x = 1$ ....

   (d) $2^3 \times 4^x = 512$ ....

Numbers Mini-Exam (2)

1   Answer the questions that follow.

   (a)   Write $2\frac{1}{4}$ as a decimal: ....

   (b)   Place the following numbers in order of size, smallest first:

$$2\frac{1}{4} \qquad 1.29^2 \qquad 2.36 \qquad 2.14 \qquad \sqrt{4.65}$$

....

2   In France a car can be bought for 30,000 euros. In America the same car can be bought for 35,000 US dollars. The exchange rates for France and America are shown below.

        France: £1 = 1.45 euros   America: £1 = \$1.67

   In which country is the car cheaper and by how much? Show all your working.

....

....

3   Write down the nth term and the 20th term of each of the following sequences:

   (a)   2   5   10   17   26 ....

....

   (b)   6   14   24   36   50   ....

....

4   When things become worth less as they get older, they are said to depreciate.

   (a)   A caravan cost £18,500 when it was new. It is now worth £12,600.

        Calculate the percentage decrease in value. ....

   (b)   Another caravan has dropped 30% in value. It is now worth £8,500.

        What was its original value? ....

5   An athlete ran 100 m in 9.92 seconds. Calculate his average speed in kilometres per hour, giving your answer to a suitable degree of accuracy.

....

....

....

Numbers Mini-Exam (2)

6 A garage is 4.6 m long and 3.2 m wide, both correct to the nearest 0.1 m.
   The height of the garage is 9 feet 3 inches, correct to the nearest 3 inches.
   Assume there are 2.5 cm to one inch.
   Find the maximum possible volume of space occupied by the garage in m³.

   ....

   ....

7 This question is about using formulas.

   (a) If $s = ut + \frac{1}{2}at^2$, calculate s when $u = 5$, $t = \frac{3}{2}$, and $a = \frac{3}{4}$.

   ....

   (b) The formula $F = \frac{9}{5}C + 32$ is used to convert temperatures in degrees Celsius (C)
        to temperatures in degrees Fahrenheit (F). A thermometer reads 36 °C.

        What is this temperature in degrees Fahrenheit?

   ....

8 Claire goes on holiday. She changes £300 into euros. (Exchange rate is £1 = 1.45 euros.)

   (a) How many euros does Claire receive? ....

   (b) She spends $\frac{3}{4}$ of her money on food. How many euros is this?

   ....

   (c) She spends 20% of the rest of her money on presents. How many euros is this?

   ....

9 There are 225 pupils in a school. Of these 105 are boys.

   (a) What fraction of the pupils are boys? Give your answer in its simplest form.

   ....

   (b) Emma goes on a charity walk of 200 miles. If she can average 12½ miles per day, how many
        days will it take her to complete the journey?

   ....

10 Write $(\sqrt{54} - \sqrt{3})^2$ in the form $a - b\sqrt{2}$, where a and b are integers.

   ....

   ....

Regular Polygons

1   The regular pentagon drawn below has been extended to form angle *r*.

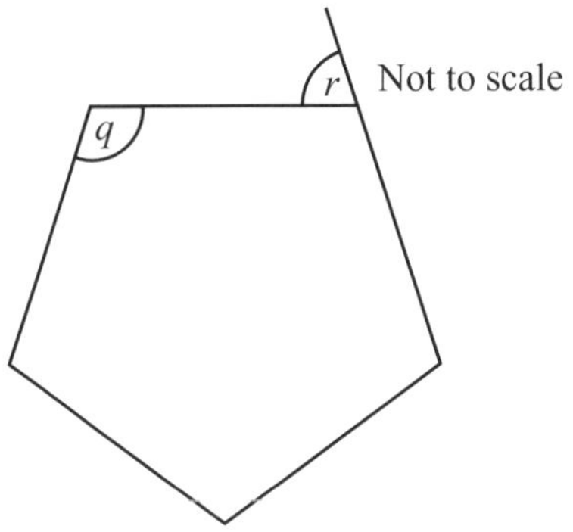

r Not to scale

q

(a)   Work out the size of angle *q*.

....

....

(b)   Work out the size of angle *r*.

....

....

2   Calculate the size of the interior angle of a regular polygon with:

(a) 9 sides

....

(b) 15 sides

....

3   A sketch of a regular octagon is shown below.

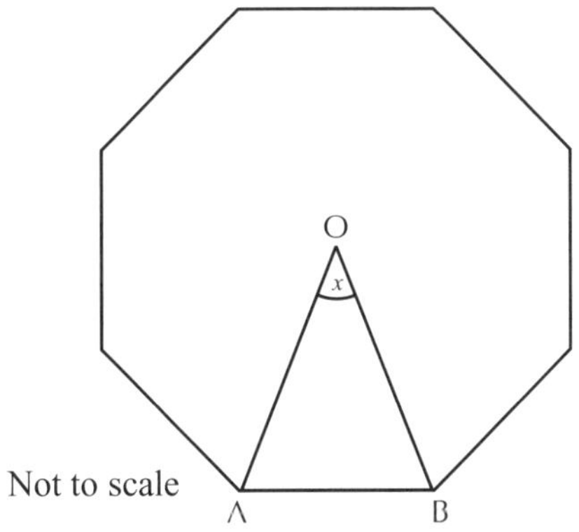

O

x

Not to scale

A   B

(a)   Work out the size of angle *x*.

....

....

....

(b)   What type of triangle is OAB?

....

4   A regular polygon has an interior angle of 150°.
How many sides does the polygon have?

....

....

....

Perimeters and Areas

1 A trapezium with an area of 168 cm² has parallel sides of lengths 6 cm and 18 cm. How far apart are the parallel sides?

....

....

2 The diagram below shows the cross-section of a swimming pool.

(a) Calculate the area of the cross-section shown. ....

....

(b) Calculate the perimeter of the cross-section shown. ....

....

3 The diagram below shows the front elevation of a building.

Calculate the area of the front elevation of the building.

....

....

....

....

4 The area of the parallelogram shown below is 105 cm².

(a) Calculate the height of the parallelogram.

....

....

....

(b) Calculate the perimeter of the parallelogram.

....

....

Perimeters and Areas

1   A circular pond has an area of 40 m². Find the radius of the pond.

    ....

    ....

2   The diagram below shows a rectangular garden area with semicircle sections at either end, one for a flowerbed and the other for a patio area. The rest is lawn.

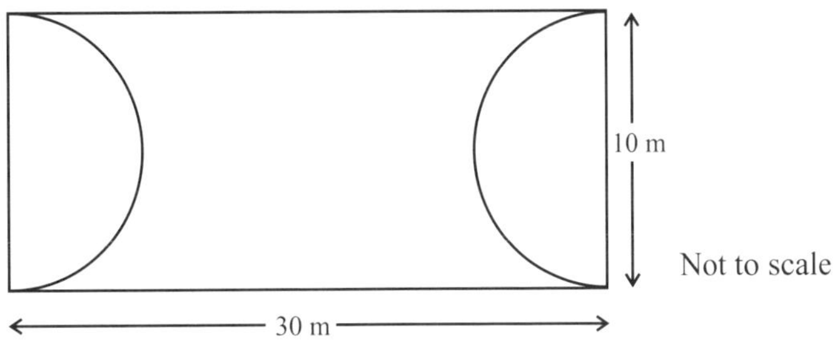

10 m

Not to scale

30 m

(a) Calculate the area of the lawn.

    ....

(b) Calculate the perimeter of the lawn.

    ....

3   The circle shown below has a radius of 12 cm and the sector subtends an angle of 50° at its centre.

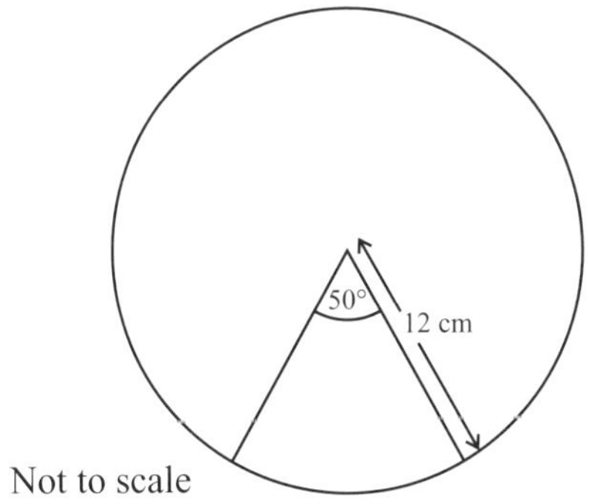

50°   12 cm

Not to scale

Find the area of the sector of the circle.

    ....

    ....

    ....

    ....

4   Look at the sector in the diagram below.

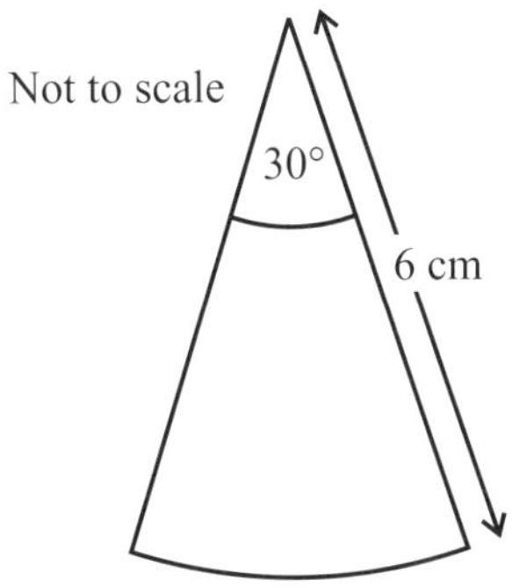

Not to scale

30°

6 cm

Find the perimeter of the sector.

    ....

    ....

    ....

    ....

Volumes

1 A diagram of a storage tunnel is shown below.

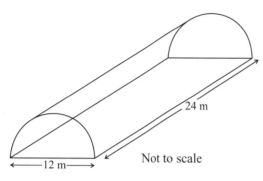

24 m

Not to scale

←—12 m—→

Find the volume, correct to 3 significant figures.

....

....

....

....

2 A cricket ball has a diameter of 75 mm.
Calculate its volume in cubic centimetres.

....

....

....

3 A pyramid has a square base with 8 cm sides, and sloping edges 10 cm in length.
Find the volume of the pyramid.

....

....

....

4 The volume of the cone shown below is 113 cm³ correct to 3 significant figures.

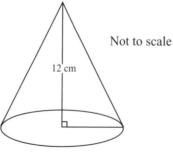

Not to scale

12 cm

Calculate the radius of the cone.

....

....

....

Geometry

1. The diagram below shows two lines intersecting two parallel lines.

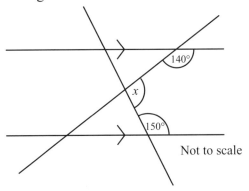

140°

x

150°

Not to scale

Find the size of angle x.

....

....

....

....

2. Look at the triangle shown below:

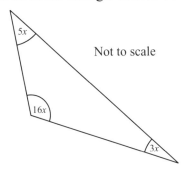

5x

Not to scale

16x

3x

Find the size of each of the angles in the triangle.

....

....

....

....

3. Look at the diagram below.

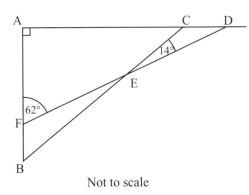

A   C   D

14°

E

62°

F

B

Not to scale

Calculate the following angles:

(a)   CDE

....

(b)   ACB

....

(c)   EBF

....

4. Look at the trapezium below.

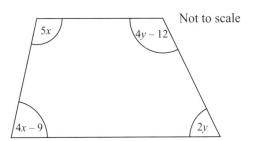

5x   4y – 12

Not to scale

4x – 9   2y

Calculate the values of x and y.

....

....

....

....

Geometry

1   Look at the diagram below.

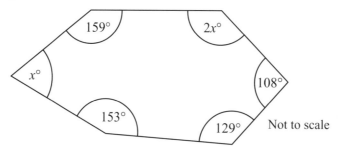

Not to scale

Calculate the size of the two unknown angles.

....

....

....

2   Calculate the sum of the interior angles of a heptagon.

....

....

....

3   The sum of the interior angles for an irregular polygon is 1260°.

(a)   How many sides does this polygon have?

....

....

(b)   What is the name of this polygon?

....

Circle Geometry

1 This diagram shows a circle with diameter AC.

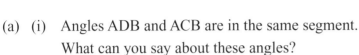

Not to scale

(a) (i) Angles ADB and ACB are in the same segment.
What can you say about these angles?

....

(ii) What is angle ABC? Explain your answer.

....

....

(iii) Explain why $x = 28°$.

....

....

(b) If AD = BD, find y.

....

....

2 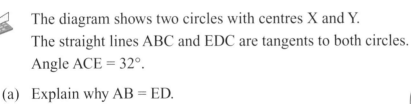 The diagram shows two circles with centres X and Y.
The straight lines ABC and EDC are tangents to both circles.
Angle ACE = 32°.

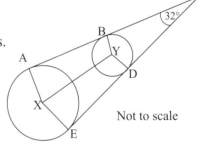

Not to scale

(a) Explain why AB = ED.

....

....

....

(b) (i) Write down the size of angles CBY and CDY. ....

(ii) Hence calculate the size of angle BYD.

....

(iii) Angles BYX and DYX are equal. How big are they? ....

(iv) Write down the size of angle XAB. ....

(v) Hence find angle AXY.

....

Circle Geometry

1 This diagram shows a circle with centre O. A, B and C are points on the circumference and angle BOC is 150°.

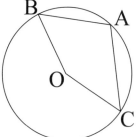

Not to scale

(a) (i) How big is the reflex angle BOC?

....

(ii) Explain why angle BAC = 105°.

....

(b) The lengths of AB and OA are equal.

(i) What can you say about triangle OBA? What is angle OBA?

....

(ii) What is angle OCA?

....

(iii) Calculate angle BCO.

....

(iv) Hence find angle BCA.

....

2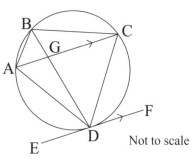

Not to scale

In the diagram on the left, the line EF is a tangent to the circle and is parallel to the chord AC.

Angle EDA = 71° and angle BAD = 100°.

(a) Write down the size of angle ACD.

....

(b) ABCD is a cyclic quadrilateral.

(i) Find the size of angle BCD. ....

(ii) Hence, show that angle BCA = 9°. ....

(c) Find the following angles, giving a reason for each answer:

Angle DAG ....

Angle ADC ....

Angle CDF ....

Angle BDA ....

Angle BDC ....

Loci and Constructions

1 The following is a scale drawing of Akela Troop scoutfield.
The council agree that the scouts can have a bonfire subject to two conditions:

    1. The bonfire must be the same distance from Stroll Lane as from Amble Road.

    2. It must be equidistant from the electricity pylons at P and Q.

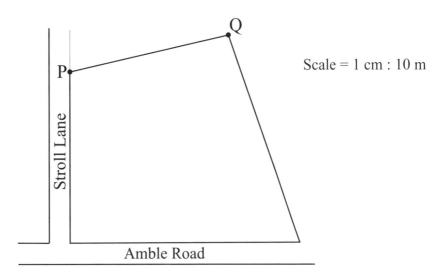

Scale = 1 cm : 10 m

Use a ruler and compasses to find and mark clearly the position of the bonfire.

2 The diagram is a scale map of the road running due north from Alchester to Burbridge.

  (a) Corway is due east of Burbridge and on a bearing of 060° from Alchester.
       Using a ruler and compasses only, find and mark Corway on the map.

Scale = 1 : 50 000

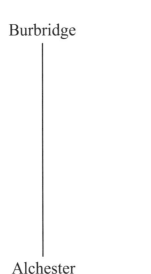

  (b) A straight canal runs from Alchester to Corway.
       A landing stage is to be built on the canal where it runs closest to Burbridge.
       Draw and measure the length of the straight path from Burbridge to the landing stage.

Congruence and Similarity

1. These triangles are
not drawn to scale:

   A 58° 57° 8 cm

   B 57° 58° 8 cm

   C 57° 58° 8 cm

   D 57° 8 cm 65°

   E 57° 58° 8 cm

   Not to scale

   Complete the following:

   Triangle ..... is congruent to triangle A because ....

   ....

   Triangle ..... is congruent to triangle B.

   Triangle ..... is congruent to neither A nor B because ....

   ....

2. These are two scale models of the same yacht.

   A 10 cm 16 cm

   B 8 cm 25 cm

   Not to scale

   Use the measurements in the diagram to calculate:

   (a) The mast height on model B ....

   ....

   (b) The depth of the hull on model A ....

   ....

3. This is a picture of Yusuf and his son. Yusuf's height is 1.81 m.
Use the picture to estimate Yusuf's son's height.

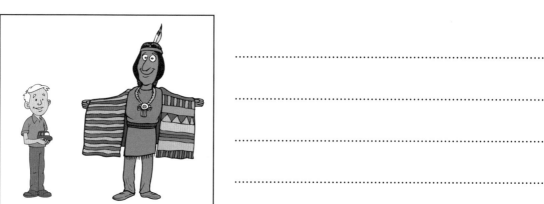

   ....

   ....

   ....

   ....

   ....

Transformations

1 Triangle ABC has been drawn on the grid below.

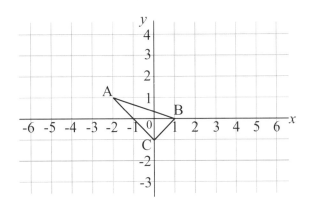

(a) Enlarge ABC by a factor of 3 about the origin. Label the image $A_1B_1C_1$.

(b) Enlarge $A_1B_1C_1$ by a factor of 0.5 about the centre (-6, -1). Label the image $A_2B_2C_2$.

(c) Describe the transformation which will map ABC directly onto $A_2B_2C_2$.

....

2 The shaded triangle has an area of 3 cm².

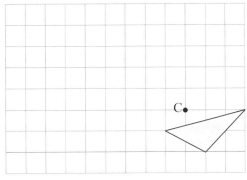

Each small square = 1 cm²

(a) Enlarge the triangle by a factor of –2 about the point C.

(b) Calculate the area of the image.

....

....

3 A spherical iron cannonball 8 cm wide weighs 2.4 kg.
A similar spherical cannonball made of the same material weighs 12 kg. Find its width.

....

....

....

....

Transformations

1 A, B and C are images of the shaded shape on the grid below.

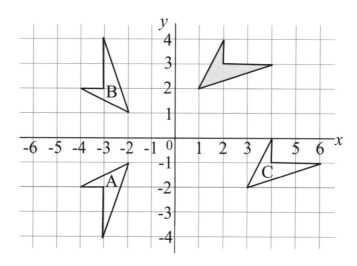

(a) Describe the transformation which will map the shaded shape onto:

(i) A ....

(ii) B ....

(iii) C ....

(b) Describe the single transformation for which C is the image of B.

....

2 An L shape has been drawn on the grid on the right.

(a) Draw the image when this shape is:

(i) reflected in the *x*-axis.
Label this image A.

(ii) rotated through 90° anticlockwise
about the point (-1, 0).
Label this image B.

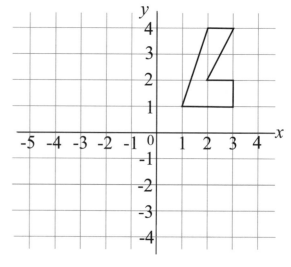

(b) What single transformation will map A onto B?

....

3D Shapes

1 Below is the cross-section of a hollow prism of length a. The cross-section consists of a circle inside an ellipse. (An ellipse is a stretched circle.)

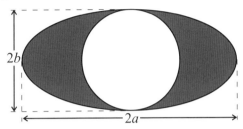

Written below are four expressions:

$$\pi ab(a - b) \qquad \pi a^2 b + 2\pi a$$

$$\pi ab - \pi b^2 \qquad \pi(a + b)$$

(a) Use three of these expressions to complete the following formulas:

Perimeter of ellipse = ...

Area of cross-section = ...

Volume of prism = ...

(b) There will be one expression you have not used.
Explain why it could not be used in any formula.

....

....

2 The piece shown below is to be cut away from this cube:

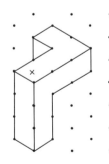

Note the position of the cross on each diagram.

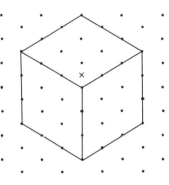

Draw the front elevation, the side elevation and the plan of the piece of the cube that will remain once the shape is cut away.

Shapes Mini-Exam (1)

1 In the diagram FAE is a tangent to the circle.
FBGD and CGA are straight lines. AD = CD.

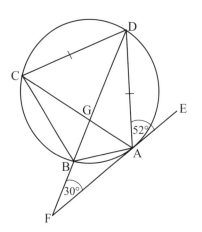

Not to scale

(a) Find angle ADC.

....

(b) Find angle FDA.

....

(c) Find angle ACB.

....

(d) Find angle BGC.

....

2 Triangle PQR has been drawn on this grid:

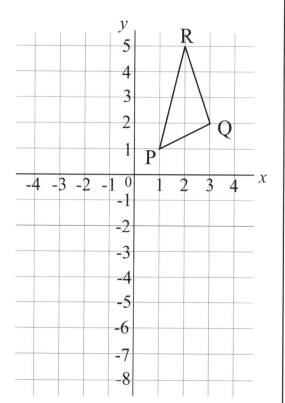

(a) Reflect PQR in the line $y = -1$.
Label the image $P_1Q_1R_1$.

(b) Reflect $P_1Q_1R_1$ in the line $y = x - 4$.
Label the image $P_2Q_2R_2$.

(c) Describe the transformation for which
PQR is the image of $P_2Q_2R_2$.

....

....

Shapes Mini-Exam (1)

3 The diagram represents three isosceles triangles.
This is because AB = AC, and BC = BD = AD.
Angle BCA = $x°$.

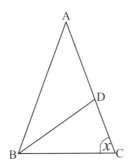

Not to scale

(a) Find angle ABD in terms of x.

....

(b) Form an equation, and hence find x.

....

4  In this diagram AB and CD are parallel.

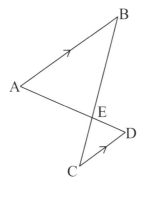

Not to scale

(a) Show that triangles ABE and DCE are similar.

....

....

(b) Given that AB = 18 cm, CD = 6 cm, CE = 5 cm and AD = 16 cm, find the lengths of:

(i) BE ....

(ii) DE ....

(c) Describe how you could transform triangle CDE onto BAE.

....

Shapes Mini-Exam (2)

1   Below is a scale plan of a goat G tethered by a 5 m rope to a shed in the corner of a large field. The goat cannot go inside the shed.

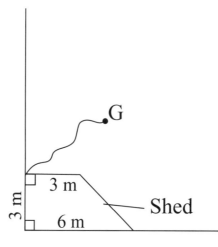

(a) Draw and shade the locus where the goat can graze.

(b) Find the area of this region.

....

....

2   The frustum shown on the right was cut from a cone.

Not to scale

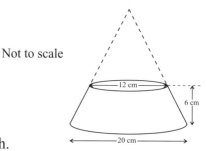

(a) Explain why the original cone must have been 15 cm high.

....

....

(b) Find the volume of the frustum. (Volume of a cone $= \frac{1}{3}\pi r^2 h$)

....

....

....

(c) What percentage of the original cone was discarded?

....

....

Shapes Mini-Exam (2)

3   Each angle of a regular polygon is 168°.
How many sides does the polygon have?

....

....

4   This diagram represents a rectangular room.

S.

3 m   Not to scale

F.

4 m

6 m

(a) Find its surface area.

....

....

(b) Sketch a net of the cuboid.

(c) A spider is at S, and a fly at F. Points S and F are midway along their respective edges.
Mark S and F on your net and hence find the shortest distance for the spider to get to the fly
along the walls of the room.

....

....

....

Density / Speed

1. A metal trophy has a volume of 900 cm³ and a mass of 3.6 kg.

    Calculate the density of the trophy. (State the units for your answer.)

    ....

    ....

2. Rachel and Bob are competing in the 400 m on Sports Day.

    Their average speeds for the race are 6.25 m/s and 25.2 km/h respectively.

    (a) Calculate which athlete runs the fastest. Show your working.

    ....

    ....

    (b) How many seconds does it take Bob to complete the race?

    ....

    ....

    (c) What distance separates the two athletes when the first of them crosses the finish line?

    ....

    ....

3. An Olympic gold medal weighs 273 g. The density of gold is 19.3 g/cm³.

    (a) What is the volume of the gold medal?

    ....

    (b) The silver medal weighs 150 g and has the same volume as the gold medal.

    What is the density of silver?

    ....

    (c) The bronze medal is made of a metal alloy which has a density of 14 g/cm³.
    All three medals have the same volume.

    What is the mass of the bronze medal?

    ....

D/T and V/T Graphs

1 The velocity/time graph below shows the details of one qualifying lap, driven by James Sprint, in the Outer Mongolian Grand Prix.

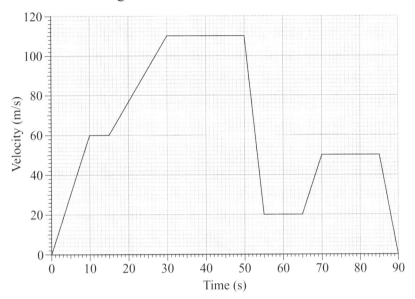

(a) What is his average acceleration during the 15 to 30 second period?
(State the units for your answer.)

....

(b) What is the meaning of the negative gradient at the end of the lap?

....

(c) What is the length of one lap?

....

2 An object is projected vertically upwards. Its distance/time graph is shown below.

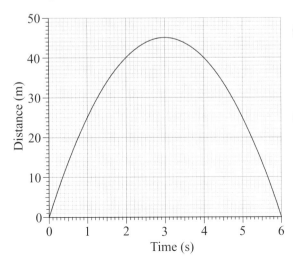

(a) At what time is the object momentarily at rest?

....

(b) Calculate the velocity of the object at time $t = 2$ seconds.

....

....

Standard Index Form

1.   Standard form is used to express very large and very small numbers.

    (a) Express the following numbers in standard form:

        (i)   12500 ....

        (ii) 0.0064 ....

        (iii) 8.6 ....

    (b) *A* and *B* are two numbers in standard form:

        $A = 4.834 \times 10^9, \quad B = 2.417 \times 10^5$

        (i)   Express *A* and *B* as ordinary numbers.

           ....

        (ii) Evaluate $A \div B$. (Give your answer in standard form.)

           ....

2.   Light travels at approximately 1.86×10^5 miles per second. Calculate the following:
(Give your answers in standard form to 3 significant figures. State the units of your answers.)

    (a) What distance will light travel in one year (365 days)?

        ....

    (b) The distance from the Earth to the Sun is approximately 9.3×10^7 miles.

        How long will it take light to travel this distance?

        ....

3.   An average grain of sand has a mass of 4.2×10^{-4} g and a volume of 8.3×10^{-2} mm³.

    Answer the following questions, giving your answers to the nearest grain.

    (a) How many grains of sand would have a combined mass of 1 gram?

        ....

    (b) How many grains of sand will it take to fill 1 cm³?

        ....

Powers and Roots

1 Evaluate the following and list them in order of size, starting with the smallest:

3^0 $\qquad$ $4^{1/2}$ $\qquad$ 5^{-3} $\qquad$ $8^{4/3}$ $\qquad$ $9^{-1.5}$ $\qquad$ $\left(\dfrac{2}{3}\right)^3$

....

2 Simplify the following:

(a) $a^5 \times a^{-3}$

....

(b) $\dfrac{x^7}{x}$

....

(c) $\dfrac{(d^3)^2}{d^4}$

....

(d) $\dfrac{(b^2)^4}{b \times b^6}$

....

3 Solve the following equations:

(a) $2^x = 32$

....

(b) $10^x = 1/100$

....

(c) $9^x = \sqrt{9}$

....

(d) $3^x = (3^4)^2 \times \dfrac{3^5}{3^{11}}$

....

Pythagoras' Theorem and Bearings

1 Find the lengths of the sides marked *x* in the following triangles:

(a)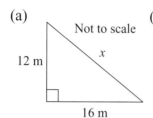

12 m   Not to scale   *x*

16 m

(b)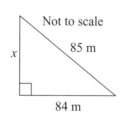

x   Not to scale   85 m

84 m

(c)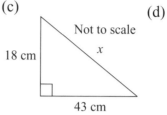

18 cm   Not to scale   *x*

43 cm

(d)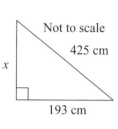

Not to scale   425 cm

x

193 cm

....

2 Two ships leave Dover at the same time.

Ship A travels due south for 40 km. Ship B travels 60 km on a bearing of 140°.

(a) Using a scale of 1 cm = 10 km, draw the journeys of the two ships in the space below and clearly mark their final positions.

N

Dover

(b) (i) Measure the final bearing of Ship B from Ship A. ....

(ii) Hence, calculate the final bearing of Ship A from Ship B. ....

3 The cuboid ABCDEFGH shown below is an insect trap.

AB = 20 cm, BC = 10 cm and AE = 5 cm.

A beetle and a wasp are caught at point A and
decide to try and escape from point G.
The beetle chooses the route A to C to G.
The wasp chooses the direct route A to G.

Calculate the distances of the two different routes.

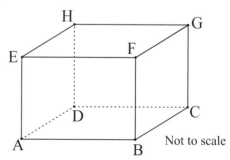

....

....

Trigonometry

1 Find the angles marked *x* in the following triangles. (Give your answers to 1 decimal place.)

(a)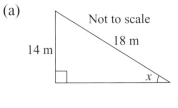

....

(b)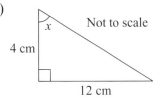

....

(c)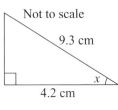

....

2 Find the sides marked *y* in the following triangles.
(Give your answers to 3 significant figures.)

(a)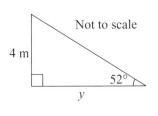

....

(b)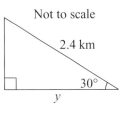

....

(c)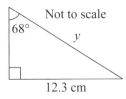

....

3 In the triangle below, AB = BC = 10 m and angle C = 34°.

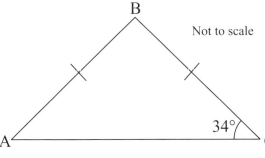

Not to scale

cos 34° = 0.829
tan 34° = 0.675
sin 34° = 0.559

(a) Calculate AC.

....

(b) Calculate the altitude of the triangle.

....

Trigonometry

1   The diagram EFGH shows a kite.

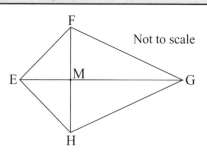

Diagonal EG bisects diagonal HF at M.

EM = 5 cm, MG = 9 cm and HF = 12 cm.

   (a) Calculate angle FGM.

   (b) Calculate angle FEH.

2   A cliff is 125 m high.

From the top of the cliff, the angles of depression of two boats, both due east, are 16° and 23° respectively.

Calculate the distance between the boats. (Give your answer to 3 significant figures.)

3   A boy at point P, on one edge of a straight stretch of river, observes two posts, Q and R, on the opposite bank. Q is directly across from P, and the distance between Q and R is 60 m.

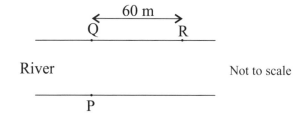

The boy estimates the angle QPR to be 40°.

Calculate the width of the river.

4   A regular hexagon is drawn such that all of its vertices are on the circumference of a circle of radius 8.5 cm.

Calculate the distance from the centre of the circle to the centre of one edge of the hexagon. (Give your answer to 2 decimal places.)

The Sine Rule

1 In the following triangles calculate the missing sides or angles marked *x*:

(a)

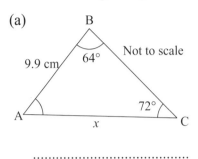

(b)

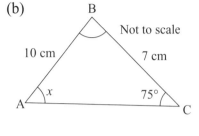

(c)

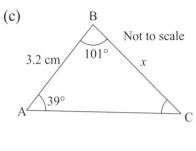

....

2 The diagram below is a functional sketch of a metal framework with some of the manufacturing information missing.

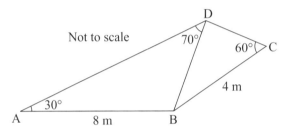

In the triangular frame BCD, calculate:

(a) BD ....

(b) Angle BDC ....

(c) DC ....

3 Two ships P and Q are positioned such that Q is 8 km from P on a bearing of 100° from P.

A third ship R is on a bearing of 160° from P and 200° from Q.

(a) Draw a sketch of this information and clearly mark the ships P, Q and R.

(b) Calculate PR. ....

(c) Calculate QR. ....

The Cosine Rule

1 In the triangle, calculate the angles marked *x* and *y*. (Give your answers to 1 decimal place.)

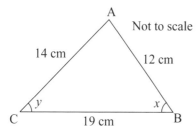

....

....

2 In the triangle to the right, calculate (AC)².

....

....

....

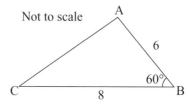

3 The diagram below shows a circular clock face with centre O. The hands OA and OB are 12 cm and 10 cm long respectively.

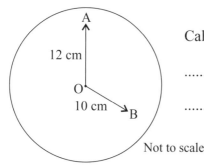

Calculate the shortest distance between A and B at 4 pm.

....

....

4 A, B and C are three landmarks on level ground.

A is 8 km due north of B. C is to the west of AB. The distance AC is 6.5 km and BC is 5 km.

(a) Draw a sketch diagram to show this information.

(b) Calculate the angle BAC. ....

(c) State the bearing of C from A. ....

Sin, Cos and Tan Graphs

1 The graph below shows $y = \sin x$ for values of x between $0°$ and $360°$.

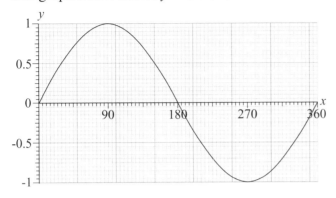

(a) Using the graph and your calculator, find all the angles between $0°$ and $360°$ that satisfy:

(i) $\sin x = 0.5$ ....

(ii) $\sin x = -0.9$ ....

(iii) $4\sin x = 1.37$ ....

(b) Complete the following table:

x	0	45	90	135	180	225	270	315	360
$\cos x$	1			-0.71	-1		0		1

(c) Plot the graph of $y = \cos x$ on the grid above and find the angles between $0°$ and $360°$ that satisfy the equation: $\sin x = \cos x$.

....

2 Indicate whether the following statements are true or false:

(a) $\cos 65°$ is positive. ....

(b) $\tan 100°$ is positive. ....

(c) $\sin 250°$ is negative. ....

(d) $\cos 330°$ is negative. ....

3 Which of the following values cannot be the sine of an angle?

0.5, 1, -0.65, 0.866, 1.2, 0.32, -1.4

....

Vectors

1 Three vectors are defined as:

$$\underline{l} = \begin{pmatrix} 4 \\ 2 \end{pmatrix} \qquad \underline{m} = \begin{pmatrix} -3 \\ 2 \end{pmatrix} \qquad \underline{n} = \begin{pmatrix} 1 \\ -4 \end{pmatrix}$$

Evaluate the following:

(a) $\underline{l} + \underline{m}$ ....

(b) $3\underline{m} - \underline{n}$ ....

(c) $2\underline{l} + \underline{m} - 2\underline{n}$ ....

2 In the diagram on the right, *ABCD* is a parallelogram.

L is the midpoint of AC, and M is the midpoint of BC.

Write in terms of $\underline{a}$ and $\underline{d}$:

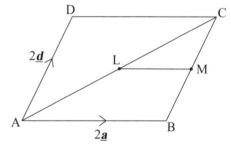

(a) **CD** ....

(b) **AC** ....

(c) **LM** ....

(d) **BL** ....

3 Look at the diagram on the right.

(a) Write in terms of $\underline{x}$ and $\underline{y}$:

(i) **SP** ....

(ii) **TQ** ....

(b) Prove that SP is parallel to TQ.

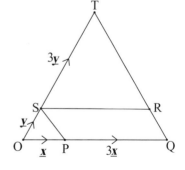

....

....

Bits and Bobs Mini-Exam (1)

1 Simplify the following expressions:

(a) $\dfrac{x^3}{x^8}$ ....

(b) $\left(x^{3/2}\right)^2$ ....

(c) $\dfrac{x^5 \times x^{-3}}{x^4 \times x^{-2}}$ ....

2 In the diagram below, X is the point on AB such that AX = 3XB.

M is the midpoint of OA and N is the midpoint of OB.

(a) Given that OA = 8**_a_** and OB = 4**_b_**, express the following in terms of **_a_** and/or **_b_**:

(i) **AB** ....

(ii) **AX** ....

(iii) **OX** ....

(iv) **MN** ....

(b) Prove that AB and MN are parallel.

....

....

3 A car is travelling at 50 m/s. It travels at this speed for 20 seconds and then slows down with constant deceleration and stops after a further 45 seconds.

(a) Plot the speed/time graph for the last 65 seconds of the journey.

(b) Calculate the gradient of the graph, and hence the deceleration, during the last 45 seconds.

....

....

(c) Calculate the total distance travelled during the last 65 seconds of the car's journey.

....

....

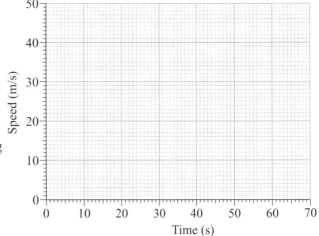

(d) Calculate the time taken to travel the first fifth of the distance.

....

Bits and Bobs Mini-Exam (1)

4 The graph below represents $y = \cos x$.

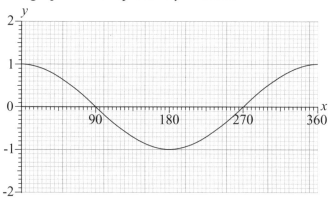

(a) Using the graph, find all the angles between 0° and 360° that satisfy the following equations:

(i) $\cos x = 0.5$

....

(ii) $\cos x = -0.2$

....

(iii) $5 \cos x = 4$

....

(b) Use what you know about the symmetry of sin *x* to complete the table below.

x	0	45	90	135	180	225	270	315	360
$2 \sin x$	0		2	1.4				-1.4	0

(i) Plot $y = 2 \sin x$ on the same axes as the graph of $y = \cos x$ (above).

(ii) Use your graph to find all the angles between 0° and 360° that satisfy: $\cos x = 2 \sin x$

....

5 *A* and *B* are two numbers in standard form. $A = 1.4 \times 10^3$, $B = 7 \times 10^{-2}$

Evaluate, giving your answers in standard form:

(a) $A \times B$ ....

(b) $B \div A$ ....

(c) $A \div B$ ....

(d) B^2 ....

6 In the diagram on the right, ABC is an equilateral triangle, with side length 20 cm.
M is the midpoint of AC and O is the centre of the inscribed circle.

Angle (°)	Sin	Cos	Tan
30	0.5	0.866	0.577
60	0.866	0.5	1.732

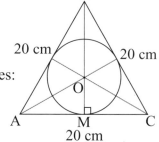

Using the trigonometric values above, calculate to 3 significant figures:

(a) The altitude of the triangle (BM).

....

(b) The diameter of the inscribed circle.

....

Bits and Bobs Mini-Exam (2)

1 In the diagram below, AB = 6 cm and CD = 11 cm. Angle BAE = 36° and angle EBD = 41°.

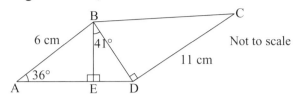

(a) Calculate BE. ....

(b) Calculate BD. ....

(c) Calculate angle BCD. ....

2 The masses of four planets are given in the table below:

Earth	Jupiter	Saturn	Venus
5.99×10^{24} kg	1.90×10^{27} kg	5.69×10^{26} kg	4.87×10^{24} kg

(a) Use data from the table to answer the following:

(i) Which of these planets has a mass which is approximately 95 times that of the Earth?

....

(ii) How many times heavier than the Earth is the planet Jupiter?

....

The radius of the Earth is approximately 6.4×10^6 m and the volume of a sphere is given by:

$V = \dfrac{4}{3} \pi \times (\text{radius})^3$

(b) Calculate the volume of the Earth correct to 3 significant figures.
(Give your answer in standard form. State the units of your answer.)

....

3 The mass of a metal statue is 0.75 kg.

The density of the metal alloy from which it is made is 12 g/cm³.

(a) Calculate the volume of the statue.

....

It is decided that the metal alloy used is not resistant enough to wear and tear and is replaced with another that has a density of 17 g/cm³. The volume of the statue must remain the same.

(b) Calculate the mass of the new statue.

....

Bits and Bobs Mini-Exam (2)

4 From a coastguard station (C), a lighthouse (L) is 12 km away on a bearing of 058° and a buoy (B) is 8 km away on a bearing of 135°.

(a) Draw a sketch diagram of this information.

(b) Calculate the distance of the lighthouse from the buoy.
(Give your answer to 2 decimal places.)

....

5 This question is about angles between 0° and 360°.

(a) Find the two solutions to the equation: $\sin x = 0.423$

....

(b) Find the smallest possible value of p which satisfies the equation: $\cos p = \cos 210°$.

....

6 A donkey and a mule set out on a 1 km race. The donkey runs at 24 km/h, but every 400 m it stops for 5 min to eat a carrot. The mule keeps going at 5 km/h.

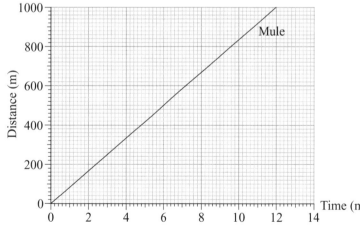

The graph on the left shows the mule's race.

(a) Plot the graph for the donkey's race on the same axes.

(b) Who wins the race and by how many seconds?

....

....

(c) After how many minutes into the race does the mule first overtake the donkey?

....

(d) What is the average speed for the donkey over the whole race? (Give your answer in m/s.)

....

Mean, Median, Mode and Range

1   For Susan's GCSE statistics project she asked 10 pupils in her class for their shoe sizes.
     These are her results: | 5, 6, 8, 7½, 5, 3, 6, 6, 4, 7 |

   (a) For this set of data write down:

        (i)   the mode ....

        (ii) the median ....

        (iii) the range ....

        (iv) the mean ....

   (b) Susan decides to include her own shoe size in the data,
        which increases the mean shoe size to 6.

        Calculate:

        (i)   Susan's shoe size.

              ....

        (ii) the mode, median and range now.

              ....

              ....

2   There are 15 boys and 13 girls in a class. In a Maths test the mean mark for the boys was b.
     In the same test the mean mark for the girls was g.
     Write down an expression for the mean mark of all 28 pupils.

     ....

     ....

3   I am thinking of 3 numbers.

                         The mean of my numbers is 22.

                         The range of my numbers is 31.

                         The median number is 29.

     Write down my 3 numbers.

     ....

     ....

     ....

Probability

1 Sanjay has two fair dice numbered 1–6. He throws them together and adds the scores.

Calculate:

(a) P(a score of 7) ....

(b) P(a total of more than 8) ....

2 Here is a 5-sided spinner. The sides are labelled 1, 2, 3, 4 and 5.
The spinner is biased. The probability that the spinner will
land on the numbers 1 to 4 is given in this table.

Number	1	2	3	4	5
Probability	0.3	0.15	0.2	0.25	

(a) Work out the probability the spinner will land on an odd number.

....

(b) I spin the spinner twice. Work out the probability that I will score 3 both times.

....

3 A box of chocolates contains 12 chocolates. 5 of the chocolates are milk chocolate,
4 are plain chocolate and 3 are white chocolate. I choose 2 chocolates at random.

1st chocolate   2nd chocolate   Outcomes

	1st chocolate	2nd chocolate	Outcomes
		Milk	MM
	Milk $\frac{5}{12}$	Plain	MP
		White	....
	Plain $\frac{4}{12}$	Milk	....
		Plain	....
		White	....
	White $\frac{3}{12}$	Milk	....
		Plain	....
		White	....

By completing the tree diagram above, calculate the probability that I pick:

(a) one milk and one white chocolate.

....

(b) at least one plain chocolate.

....

Frequency Tables

1 The table shows the number of pets owned by each pupil in class 7F.

Number of pets	0	1	2	3	4	5
Frequency	8	3	5	8	4	1

(a) How many pupils are there in class 7F?

....

(b) What is the mean number of pets per pupil?

....

2 For her GCSE homework Vanessa collected information about the number of text messages pupils in her school sent each day. She recorded her results in the frequency table below.

Number of messages	0	2	3	5	7	8	10
Frequency	2	5	8	6	5	2	1
Number × frequency			24			16	

(a) Complete the frequency table.

(b) Use the table to calculate:

   (i) the mean number of text messages sent.

   ....

   ....

   (ii) the modal number of text messages sent.

   ....

   ....

   (iii) the median number of text messages sent.

   ....

   ....

Grouped Frequency Tables

1 32 pupils in a class sat an exam in Science.
The distribution of their marks is given in the table below.

Exam mark	11-20	21-30	31-40	41-50	51-60	61-70
Frequency	2	5	7	8	4	6
Mid-interval value						
Frequency × mid-interval value						

(a) Complete the table.

(b) Use the table to find:

    (i)   the modal group. ....

    (ii) the group which contains the median.

       ....

    (iii) an estimate of the mean (give your answer to 1 decimal place).

       ....

2 During a science experiment 10 seeds were planted and their growth measured in cm
after 12 days. The results were recorded in the table below.

Growth in cm	0-2	3-5	6-8	9-11
Number of plants	2	4	3	1

Use the table to find:

(a) the group which contains the median.

    ....

(b) the modal class.

    ....

(c) an estimate of the mean.

    ....

(d) Explain why you can only find an "estimate".

    ....

    ....

Cumulative Frequency

1   120 pupils in a year group sit an examination at the end of the year.
Their results are given in the table below.

Exam mark (%)	0-20	21-30	31-40	41-50	51-60	61-70	71-80	81-100
Frequency	3	10	12	24	42	16	9	4

(a) Complete the cumulative frequency table below and use it to
draw a cumulative frequency curve on the graph paper.

Exam mark (%)	≤20.5	≤30.5	≤40.5	≤50.5	≤60.5	≤70.5	≤80.5	≤100.5
Cumulative Frequency								

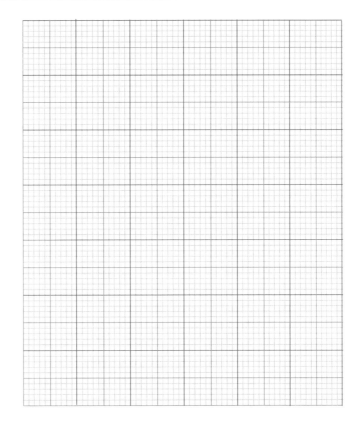

Use your curve to find:

(b) (i)   The median mark ....   (ii)   The lower quartile ....

(iii) The upper quartile ....   (iv)   The inter-quartile range ....

(c) Use your results from part (b) to draw a box plot to illustrate the data.

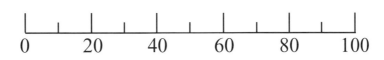

Histograms and Frequency Density

1 The scores of individual pupils in an exam are given below:

75, 52, 50, 73, 58, 50, 61, 55, 43, 45, 65

(a) Draw a stem and leaf diagram for this data.

(b) Find the range of the results from your diagram.

....

2 The histogram shows the number of minutes pupils watch television for one evening.

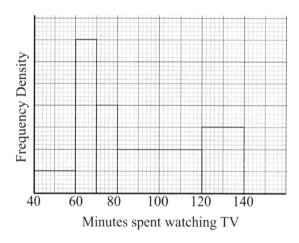

Minutes spent watching TV

20 pupils watched between 40 and 60 minutes.

(a) Use the histogram to complete this table.

Number of minutes watched	Frequency
$40 \leq m < 60$	20
$60 \leq m < 70$	
$70 \leq m < 80$	
$80 \leq m < 120$	
$120 \leq m < 140$	

(b) How many pupils took part in the survey?

....

Correlation, Dispersion and Spread

1 What type of correlation would you expect to see if you drew a scatter graph to compare:

(a) the age of a car and its value? ....

(b) hand span and index finger length? ....

(c) shoe size and number of pets? ....

2 As part of his GCSE project work, Sam decided to ask 10 primary school pupils how old they were and what time they were sent to bed. He recorded his results in the table below.

Age in years	6	9	9	6	8	7	9	7	8	8
Bedtime	7.30	8.00	8.30	7.00	8.00	7.30	9.00	8.00	8.30	7.30

(a) Draw a scatter graph to show this information.

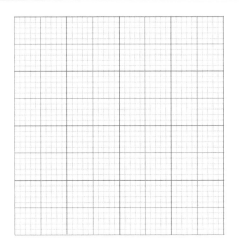

(b) Sam's little brother is 6½ years old. According to your graph, what time should he expect to go to bed? ....

3 A simple test of 10 maths questions was given to all pupils moving to a secondary school. A histogram of the results is shown below.

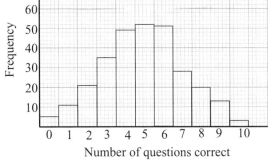

(a) Comment on the shape of the distribution.

....

(b) Estimate the value of the mean.

....

Sampling Methods

1 Susie is investigating the heights of pupils in her school in order to advise the company that make the school uniform. There are 720 pupils in the school.

Year	7	8	9	10	11
Number of pupils	167	162	150	125	116

(a) Describe:

(i) how a random sample of 100 students could be chosen.

....

....

(ii) how a stratified random sample of 100 students could be chosen, stating how many students would come from each year group.

....

....

....

....

(b) What additional information would she need in order to carry out a quota sample?

....

2 A new football club wants to see if there is any trend in its attendance figures.

Week	1	2	3	4	5	6	7	8	9	10
Members	32	25	43	28	42	32	44	46	30	45

(a) Calculate the four-weekly moving averages.

....

....

....

(b) Describe the trend you can see in the attendance figures.

....

....

Statistics Mini-Exam (1)

1 The stem and leaf diagram shows the amount of rainfall in mm that fell during a period of 14 days one November.

Key: 1 | 2 = 12 mm

```
0 | 1  2  2  3  4
1 | 2  3  5  5
2 | 0  2  2  2  3
```

(a)   Write down the modal value. ....

(b)   Write down the median value. ....

(c)   Calculate the range of the data. ....

(d)   Calculate the mean value. ....

....

2 200 pupils sat an entrance exam. The cumulative frequency curve shows the marks they obtained.

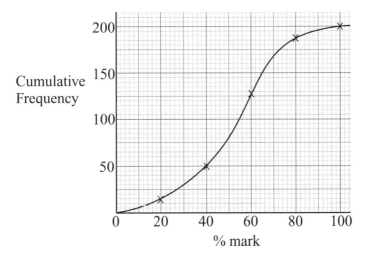

Use the graph to find:

(a) (i)   the median mark. ....

(ii) the lower quartile. ....

(iii) the upper quartile. ....

(iv) the inter-quartile range. ....

(b)   If the pass mark was 64 marks, estimate how many pupils passed.

....

Statistics Mini-Exam (1)

3 In a particular class in school 15 pupils study both Spanish and Italian.
Their end of year exam results are given in the table below.

Spanish (%)	42	32	61	41	53	72	65	50	80	43	66	38	23	12	72
Italian (%)	54	43	70	44	60	76	72	62	91	52	71	42	38	24	81

(a) Draw a scatter diagram to illustrate this data.

(b) Describe the correlation you can see in your diagram. ....

(c) Ahmed was absent for his Spanish exam but scored 66% for his Italian.
Estimate the mark he might have obtained for Spanish. ....

4 A school contains 800 pupils.
The number of pupils in each year group is given in the table below.

Year	7	8	9	10	11
Number of pupils	184	160	136	176	144

A stratified sample of 100 pupils is to be taken. How many pupils should be picked from each year group?

....

....

....

Statistics Mini-Exam (2)

1 The weekly wages of 70 part-time workers at a factory are given in the table.

Wages (£)	Number of employees
70 – 79	3
80 – 89	11
90 – 99	8
100 – 109	15
110 – 119	24
120 – 129	7
130 – 139	2

(a) Use the table to write down:

(i) the group containing the modal wage. ....

(ii) the group that contains the median wage.

....

(b) Calculate an estimate of the mean wage.

....

....

2 On my way to work in the morning the probability that I stop to buy a newspaper is 0.7.
If I stop to buy the paper the probability that I am late for work is 0.4.
On other mornings the probability that I am late for work is 0.15.

(a) Complete the tree diagram to illustrate this situation.

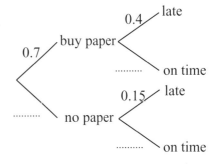

(b) Use the tree diagram to calculate:

(i) the probability that I am on time for work and I have bought a newspaper.

....

(ii) the probability that I am late for work.

....

(c) If I am at work for 200 days a year, how many days can I expect to be late?

....

Statistics Mini-Exam (2)

3 The temperature in London was recorded for 15 days one July.
The highest daily temperature was recorded and the results are given below.

Day	1	2	3	4	5	6	7	8	9	10	11	12	13	14	15
Temp (°C)	28	26	24	27	19	22	23	23	21	20	17	19	25	25	24

(a) Draw a box plot of this data, marking clearly the value of the median and the lower and upper quartiles.

(b) Calculate the mean of the data.

....

....

4 The histogram shows the weight of apples which fell from a tree.
There were 8 apples in the 30-50 g group.

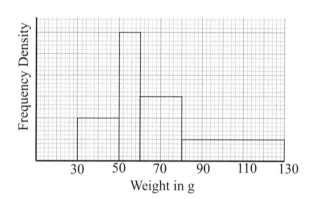

Use the histogram to find the total number of apples which fell.

....

....

5 During bad weather, the probability that I have an accident in my car on a given day is $\frac{1}{40}$.

In fine weather this reduces to $\frac{1}{200}$. The probability of bad weather on any day is $\frac{1}{5}$.

Calculate P(I have a car accident on a given day).

....

....

Straight Line Graphs

1 Draw and label the following graphs on the axes below:

$y = -1$

$x = 0$

$x = 2$

$y = x$

$y = -2x$

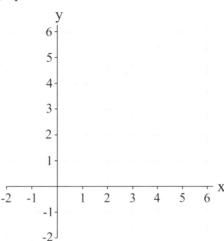

2 The box below contains the equations of some lines and curves.

Tick the ones that are equations of straight lines.

$x + y = 0$	$y = 2x^2$	$y = \frac{1}{2}x - 2$
$xy = 8$	$x = 2$	$2y + 3x = 2$
$y^2 + x^3 = 2$	$y = \frac{x}{3}$	$y = \frac{3}{x}$

3 Draw and label these graphs on the axes below:

$2y + x = 7$

$y = 2x + 3$

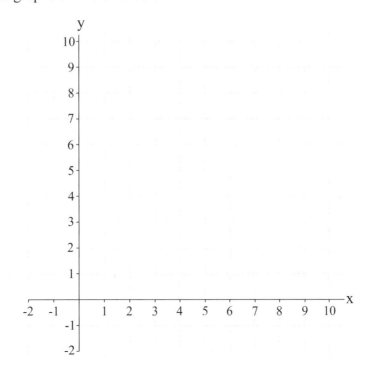

Straight Line Graphs

1 This question is about straight line graphs.

(a) Find the gradient and the *y*-intercept for each of the following straight line graphs:

(i) $y = 3x + 2$

....

(ii) $y = 5 - x$

....

(iii) $2x + y = 7$

....

(iv) $x - 5y - 2 = 0$

....

(b) Use your answers to parts (i) and (ii) above to sketch the graphs of $y = 3x + 2$ and $y = 5 - x$.

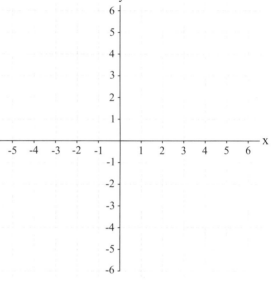

2 Match the lines A, B, C and D in the diagram to the equations below:

$y = 4 + x$ ......

$x + y = 6$ ......

$y = 2x$ ......

$3y - x = 2$ ......

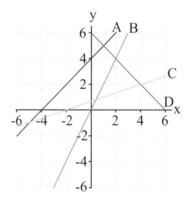

3 Look at the straight line graph shown in the diagram.

(a) Find the equation of the straight line graph.

....

(b) A straight line graph has the same gradient as the one in part (a), but goes through the point (0, -1).

(i) Write down the equation of this graph.

....

(ii) Sketch the graph on the axes on the right.

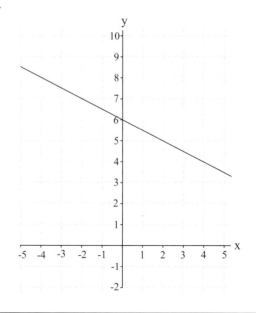

Linear Programming

1 The KattyKit Cat Food Company produces cat food in large and small tins, and can always sell as much cat food as it makes.

The company only has the capacity to produce 200 tins in total per day.

It also insists that stores take delivery of no more than four times as many large tins as small tins.

L is the number of large tins produced in a day and S is the number of small tins.

(a) Write down two inequalities that L and S must satisfy.

....

(b) Show on a graph the region in which both inequalities are satisfied. Use the axes below.

(c) The company sells the large tins of cat food for 45p, and the small tins for 25p.

Use your graph to find the number of tins of each size KattyKit should make in order to maximise their income.
What is this maximum daily income?

....

2 Yasmin has 50p to spend on sweets.

She is going to have some Kola Kubes and some Minty Munches.

Kola Kubes cost 2p each and Minty Munches cost 3p each.

Yasmin wants to have at least 10 Kola Kubes.

She also wants at least half as many Minty Munches as Kola Kubes.

(a) Using K to represent the number of Kola Kubes and M to represent the number of Minty Munches, write down 3 inequalities that K and M must satisfy.

....

....

....

(b) Show on a graph the region in which all of your inequalities are satisfied.

(c) Use your graph to find the maximum number of sweets that Yasmin can buy.

....

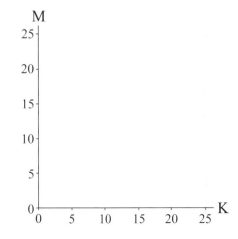

Coordinates

1   Point P has coordinates (6, 5) and point Q has coordinates (2, -1).

Find the length of PQ, giving your answer correct to two decimal places.

....

....

2   Point A has coordinates (2, 5, 7).

Point B has coordinates (0, 3, 8).

Point C has coordinates (3, 7, 5).

(a) Find the lengths of lines AB and AC.

....

....

(b) What can you say about triangle ABC?

....

3   Point P has coordinates (6, 2) and point Q has coordinates (-4, 1).

(a) Find the coordinates of the midpoint of PQ.

....

....

Point R has coordinates (a, b).

(b) The midpoint of PR is (3, 5).

Find the values of a and b.

....

....

Solving Equations Using Graphs

1 A ball is thrown upwards from the top of a cliff, so that it falls down to the sea below.

The cliff is 50 m high.

The graph shows the height h of the ball from sea level, t seconds after it has been thrown.

From the graph, find:

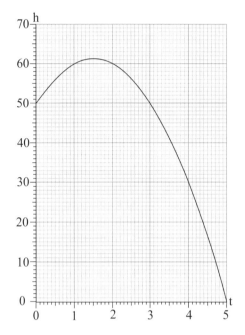

(a) the time taken for the ball to fall to sea level.

....

(b) the height of the ball after 4 seconds.

....

(c) the time when the ball is again at the same height as the cliff.

....

(d) the maximum height of the ball above the ground, and the time at which it reaches this height.

....

2 This question is about the function $y = x^3 - 4x^2 + 4$.

(a) Complete the table below. The first few have been done for you.

x	-1	-0.5	0	0.5	1	1.5	2	2.5	3	3.5	4
$x^3 - 4x^2 + 4$	-1	2.875	4	3.125	1	-1.625	-4				

(b) Use your table to draw the graph of $y = x^3 - 4x^2 + 4$ on the axes on the right.

(c) Using your graph or otherwise, estimate:

(i) the value of y when $x = 3.2$.

....

(ii) the value(s) of x when $y = 0$.

....

....

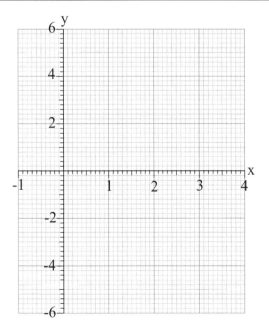

Simultaneous Equations and Graphs

1   The diagram shows part of the graph of $y = 4x - x^2$.

   (a) Using the same axes,
        draw the graph of $y = 5x - 2$.

   (b) Use the graphs to find the solution(s)
        to the simultaneous equations:

        $y = 5x - 2$

        $y = 4x - x^2$

        ....

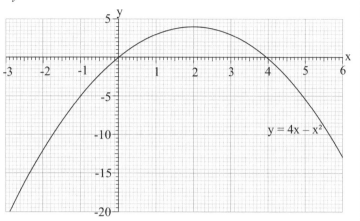

2   On the axes below, draw suitable graphs and hence obtain the solution
   of the simultaneous equations:

   $4y + 3x = 25$

   $2y - x = 5$

   ....

   ....

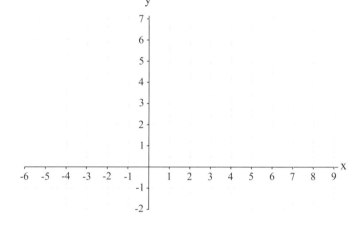

3   The diagram shows the graphs of $y = \dfrac{6}{x - 2}$ and $y = 2x - 5$.

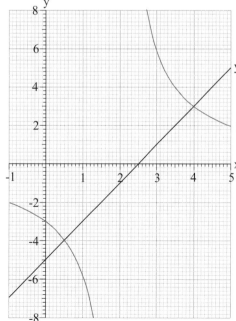

   Using these graphs, write down the
   solution(s) of the equation:

   $6 = (x - 2)(2x - 5)$

   ....

Tangents and Gradients

1 The graph below shows the speed of a train travelling between two stations.

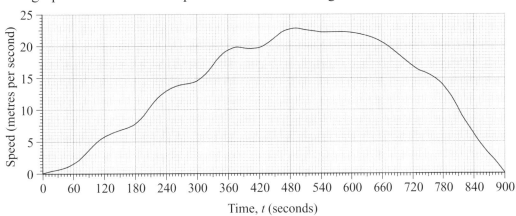

(a) Draw a tangent to the graph at the point 4 minutes after the train leaves the first station. Hence find the gradient of the graph at that point.

....

(b) What does the gradient of the graph represent here?

....

(c) Explain what the total area under the graph between $t = 0$ and $t = 900$ represents.

....

2 The diagram below shows the graph of $y = x^3 - 3x^2 + 2x + 5$.

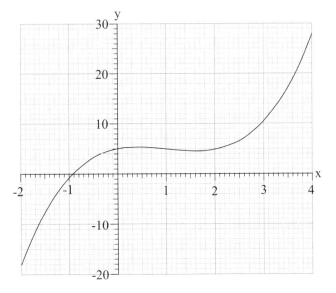

(a) Draw a tangent to the graph at the point where $x = 3$. Hence find its gradient at that point.

....

(b) Find the coordinates of another point on the graph which has the same gradient.

....

68

Finding Equations from Graphs

1 The graph on the right is of the form $y = a - bx^2$.

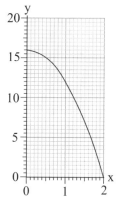

(a) Write down the coordinates of the points where the graph crosses:

(i) the x-axis. ....

(ii) the y-axis. ....

(b) Hence find the equation of the curve.

....

2 Bilal had to learn the stopping distances of a car at various speeds for his driving theory test.

Instead of learning a table of values, he thought it would be easier to find a formula for them.

He drew this graph from his table of values.

Bilal thought the graph was of the form $d = av + bv^2$.

Find the values of a and b.

....

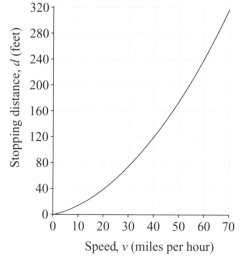

3 Look at the diagram below.

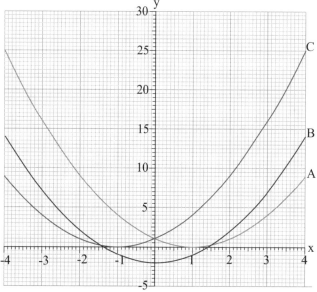

Each of these graphs can be obtained from the graph of $y = x^2$ by a single translation.

(a) Describe the translation for each graph.

....

....

....

....

....

(b) Use your answers to (a) to give the equation of each graph.

....

Finding Equations from Graphs

1 The diagram below shows the graph of $y = ax^3 + b$.

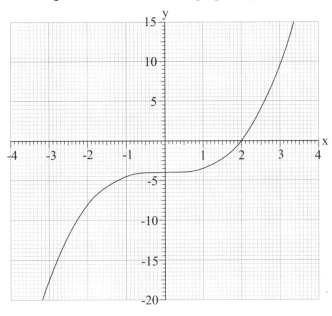

Find the values of a and b.

....

2 The diagram on the right shows the graph of $y = ax^3 - bx^2 + c$.

(a) Explain why $c = 3$.

....

....

(b) Use the point (1, 4) to show that $a - b = 1$.

....

(c) Use the point (-1, 0) to find another equation connecting a and b.

....

(d) Find the values of a and b.

....

....

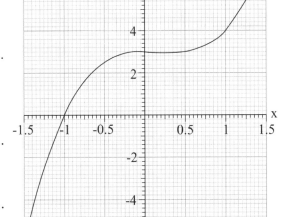

Finding Equations from Graphs

1 The diagram on the right shows the graph of $y = \dfrac{k}{x}$.

Find the value of k.

....

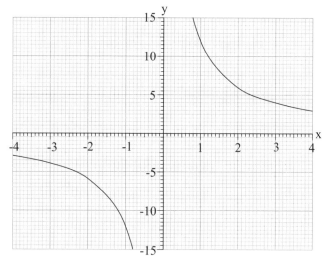

2 The diagram below shows the graph of $y = \dfrac{a}{x} + b$.

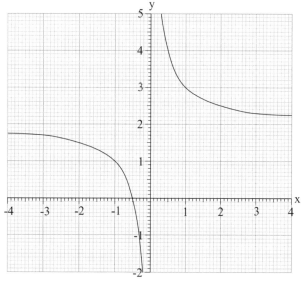

(a) Use the point $(1, 3)$ to show that $a + b = 3$.

....

(b) Find another equation connecting a and b.

....

(c) Find the values of a and b.

....

(d) State the transformation needed to obtain this graph from the graph of $y = \dfrac{1}{x}$.

....

3 The diagram on the right shows the graph of $y = \dfrac{1}{x}$.

On the same diagram, sketch and label the graphs of $\dfrac{1}{x} - 2$ and $\dfrac{1}{x-2}$.

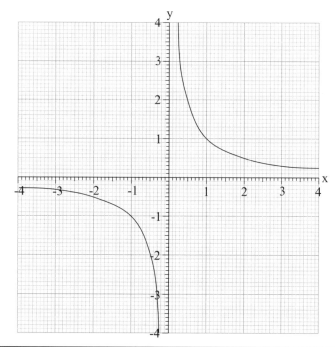

Finding Equations from Graphs

1 The growth of a colony of bacteria over time can be modelled using the equation:

$y = pq^x$

The graph below shows the growth of a colony of bacteria.

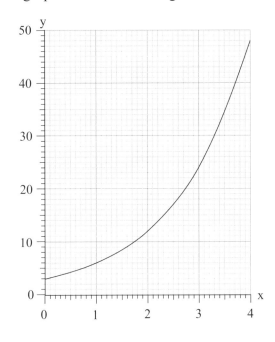

Find the values of p and q.

....

2 The diagram shows the graph of $y = a^x + b$.

(a) Use the point $(0, 4)$ to show that $b = 3$.

....

....

(b) Find the value of a.

....

....

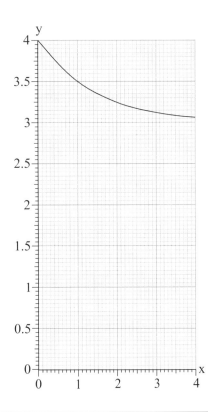

Finding Equations from Graphs

1   The diagram below shows the graph of $y = a + b \sin kx$.

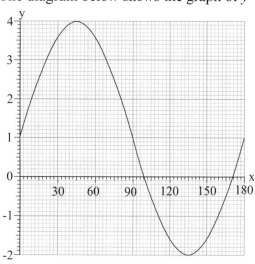

(a)   Find the value of a.

....

(b)   Find the value of k.

....

(c)   Find the value of b.

....

2   The diagram on the right shows the graph of $y = \cos x$ for x between $0°$ and $360°$.

On the same axes, sketch the graphs of:

(a) $y = \cos 2x$

(b) $y = \cos x + 2$

(c) $y = 2 \cos x$

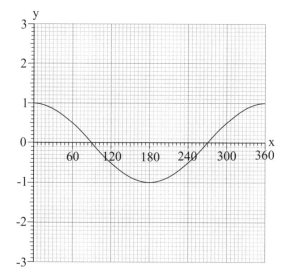

3   A curve has equation $y = a + \tan bx$.

(a) It goes through the point $(0, 2)$.

Find the value of a.

....

(b) The curve also goes through the point $(9, 3)$.

(i) Show that $\tan 9b = 1$.

....

(ii) Find the value of b.

....

Graphs Mini-Exam (1)

1 There are two taxi firms in Anytown. The two firms work out their charges as shown below:

Tel's Taxis: £1 basic fee + 20p per 100 metres

Kev's Kabs: No basic fee, but 30p per 100 metres

(a) Draw and label lines to represent these charges on the axes below.

(b) Explain what is represented by:

   (i) the gradient of the lines.

   ....

   ....

   (ii) the intercept on the *y*-axis.

   ....

   ....

(c) Use your graph to find the distance for which the two companies charge the same.

   ....

(d) Someone asks your advice on which taxi firm to use. Write down what you would tell them.

   ....

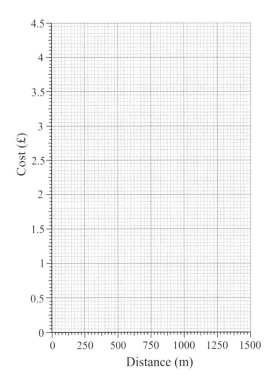

2 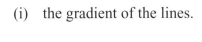 The diagram below shows the curve $y = x^2$.

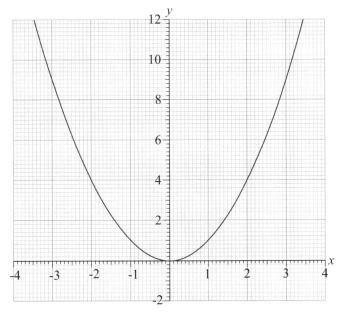

(a) On the same axes, draw the curve $y = (x - 2)^2$.

(b) Use your graphs to write down the point at which $x^2 = (x - 2)^2$.

   ....

   Look at the gradient of $y = x^2$ at the point $(1, 1)$.

(c) Find the coordinates of a point on $y = (x - 2)^2$ where the curve has the same gradient.

   ....

Graphs Mini-Exam (1)

3 A printing firm quotes these figures for printing different numbers of leaflets:

Number of leaflets	100	200	500	1000	2000	5000
Price per leaflet	£1	50p	20p	10p	5p	2p

(a) Plot these points on the axes below and draw a smooth curve through them.

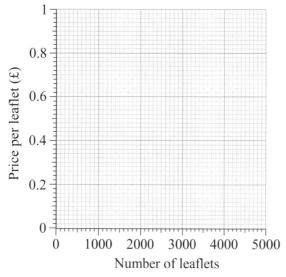

(b) Use your graph to work out the likely cost per leaflet for 2500 leaflets.

....

(c) The curve you have drawn has the equation $P = \dfrac{k}{N}$, where P = price in pounds per leaflet, and N = number of leaflets. Find the value of k.

....

....

4 Dina is planning a barbecue. She is going to buy burgers and sausages.
She wants to have at least as many burgers as sausages.
She must have at least 8 sausages for her friends who do not like burgers.
Burgers cost 25p each and sausages 20p each. She has a total of £6 to spend.

Let B stand for the number of burgers and S for the number of sausages.

(a) Use the information above to write down three inequalities that B and S must satisfy.

....

(b) On the axes on the right, shade the region which represents the possible numbers of burgers and sausages Dina can buy.

(c) What is the maximum number of items (burgers and sausages together) that she can buy?

....

....

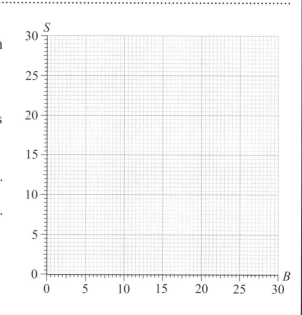

Graphs Mini-Exam (2)

1 Answer the question below about the graph of $y = x^3 - 2x^2 + x + 1$.

(a) Complete the table of values:

x	-3	-2	-1	0	1	2	3
x^3							
$-2x^2$							

(b) Using your table to help you, draw the graph of $y = x^3 - 2x^2 + x + 1$ on the axes below.

(c) Use your graph to find the value(s) of x for which $y = -5$.

....

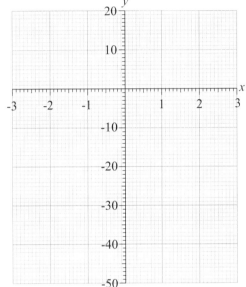

(d) Draw a tangent to your curve at the point where $x = -2$, and use it to find the gradient of the curve.

....

....

2 Points P and Q are plotted on graph paper.

Point P is (3, 7). Point Q is (2, 9).

(a) Find:

(i) the length of PQ (give your answer to 2 decimal places).

....

(ii) the midpoint of PQ. ....

(b) Find the gradient of PQ. ....

(c) If the line PQ is extended, it goes through the point R, with coordinates $(0, c)$.

(i) What is the gradient of QR?

....

(ii) Use your answers to (b) and (c) (i) to find c.

....

(d) Write down the equation of the line that goes through P and Q.

....

Section Five

Graphs Mini-Exam (2)

3 The diagram below shows a straight line.

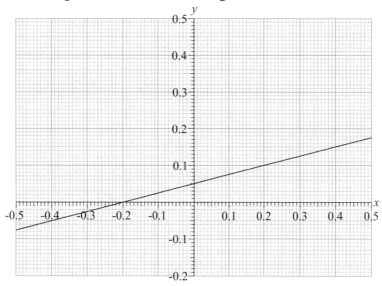

(a) Find the equation of the line.

....

....

(b) On the same axes, draw the line $2x + y = 0.5$.

(c) Write down:

  (i) the intersection point of these two lines. ....

  (ii) a pair of simultaneous equations to which this point gives the solution.

  ....

4 Sanjay did a physics experiment on pendulums. He took pendulums of various lengths, and noted the time it took for each pendulum to complete a full swing backwards and forwards. Here are his results:

Length (L) / metres	0.2	0.4	0.6	0.8	1.0	1.2	1.4	1.6	1.8	2.0
Time (T) / seconds	0.90	1.27	1.55	1.80	2.01	2.20	2.37	2.54	2.69	2.84

(a) Plot these points on the graph paper below and connect them with a smooth curve.

(b) Use your graph to find:

  (i) the length of a pendulum that takes 1.1 seconds for a full swing backwards and forwards.

  ....

  (ii) the time a pendulum of length 0.9 m takes for a full swing backwards and forwards.

  ....

  Sanjay thinks that this curve is of the form $T = a\sqrt{L}$.

(c) Find a.

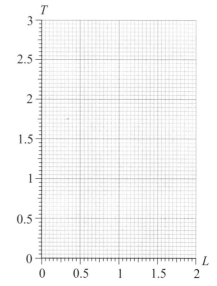

  ....

Basic Algebra

1   Complete the diagram by writing expressions in the empty boxes:

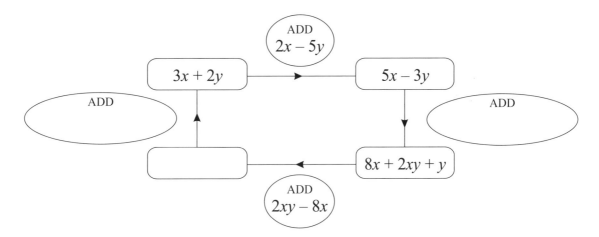

2 Write **one** term in each empty space to make the equation correct:

(a) $2(3x + 5) = 6x +$ ....

(b) ....$(4a -$ ....$) = 12a^2 - 6a$

(c) $3x -$ .... $+ 4(2x + 5) =$ .... $+ 18$

(d) $6($................................. $- 4) - (d -$ ....$) = 17d - 22$

3 Multiply out the brackets in these expressions. Simplify your answers as much as possible.

(a) $5x - 3(x - 1)$ ....

(b) $4a(b + 1) + b(2a - 1)$ ....

(c) $8(3 - 2p) - 2(p - 3)$ ....

(d) $(2t - 5)(3t + 4)$ ....

(e) $(x + 3)^2$ ....

Basic Algebra

1 Write a term in each empty space to complete the factorisations below:

(a) $8b - 12 =$ ....$(2b -$ ....$)$

(b) $2a^2 +$ .... $= 2a($.............................. $+ 3b)$

(c) $9d^2e -$ .... $+ 15de^2f = 3de($.............................. $- e^2 +$ ....$)$

(d) .... $- 16 = (x -$ ....$)(x +$ ....$)$

2 Factorise the following three expressions as much as possible:

(a) $15x^2 - 6xy$ = ... (.......................................)

(b) $12x^2 + 10x$ = ... (.......................................)

(c) $8x - 12xy$ = ... (.......................................)

3 Simplify the following as much as possible:

(a) $\dfrac{4a \times 3ab}{6ab^2}$

....

....

(b) $\dfrac{10x}{3+x} \div \dfrac{4}{5(3+x)}$

....

....

(c) $\dfrac{2}{3} + \dfrac{m-2n}{m+3n}$

....

....

(d) $\dfrac{y^2-1}{3y+3}$

....

....

Solving Equations

1 Apply the step shown to each equation, then solve the result.

(a) (i) Gather all the terms involving y on one side: $5 + 3y = y - 11$

....

(ii) Now solve for y.

....

(b) (i) Square both sides: $\sqrt{(3x + 10)} = 7$

....

(ii) Now solve for x.

....

(c) (i) Multiply by terms on the bottom line of the fraction: $\dfrac{a}{2a + 3} - 5 = 2$

....

(ii) Now solve for a.

....

....

2 Solve these equations:

(a) $\dfrac{4 - 3d}{5d} + 7 = 6$ ....

....

....

(b) $\sqrt{2(3h + 5)} = 5$ ....

....

....

(c) $3x^2 = 12$ ....

....

Rearranging Formulas

1 Follow the instructions given for each equation below:

   (a) Collect the terms with y in on the left-hand side of the equation:

      $x^2 + 2xy = 3y + 4$ $2xy -$ .... $= 4 -$ ....

   (b) Square both sides of the equation:

      $T = 2\pi\sqrt{h}$ $T^2 =$ ....

   (c) Multiply by the term on the bottom line of the fraction:

      $B = \dfrac{3C + 2}{5B} + 2C^2$ .... $= 3C + 2 +$ ....

2 Complete the rearrangement of this formula, making n the subject, by filling in the blanks:

$$2n = 3m + \frac{5(2m - n)}{3k}$$

   Step 1 — Multiply the equation by $3k$:   ....

   Step 2 — Multiply out any brackets: ....

   Step 3 — Collect terms involving n on the left: ....

   Step 4 — .... $n($.....................$) =$ ....

   Step 5 — Make n the subject: $n =$ ....

3 Rearrange these formulas to make the letter in the brackets the subject:

   (a) $s = \dfrac{1}{2}gt^2$ (t) ....

     ....

   (b) $a + y = \dfrac{b - y}{a}$ (y) ....

     ....

   (c) $x = \sqrt{\dfrac{(1 + n)}{(1 - n)}}$ (n) ....

     ....

Inequalities

1 Complete the table of inequalities for the INTEGER values of x, y, z and p.

Statement	Inequality	Possible values
x is between -3 and $+5$, but never equal to either number	$-3 < x < 5$	
	$2 < y < 8$	
		$-5, -4, -3, -2, -1, 0$
	$p^2 < 16$	

2 Solve the following inequalities:

(a) $3x \leq 5 + 2x$ ....

(b) $10 < 2x - 6$ ....

(c) $4x + 1 > x - 5$ ....

(d) $\dfrac{2x}{5} \leq 3$ ....

3 Solve these double inequalities. Treat each side as a separate inequality.

(a) $10 \leq 2x \leq x + 9$ ....

....

(b) $3 < 3x - 1 < 2x + 7$ ....

....

(c) $4x + 1 < 5x < 3(x + 2)$ ....

....

Direct and Inverse Proportion

1. This question is about quantities that are directly and inversely proportional to each other.

    (a) The quantities A and B are directly proportional. Complete the table of values.

A	3	6			81	
B	5		20	30		65

    (b) P is inversely proportional to Q. Complete the table of values.

P	5	10		2		
Q	20		4		40	200

2. The cost of petrol is directly proportional to the quantity bought.

    (a) If 9 litres costs £6.48:

        (i) How much does 1 litre cost? ....

        (ii) How much does 20 litres cost? ....

    (b) Use the same method to find the mass of 9 cm of wire given that 15 cm has a mass of 19 g.

    ....

    (c) A train travels 80 km in 100 minutes.

        (i) At the same speed, how long does it take to travel 1 km?

        ....

        (ii) How far will it travel in 2 hours 30 minutes?

        ....

3. Work out the answers to these inverse proportion questions:

    (a) The time it takes to harvest the crop in a field is inversely proportional to the number of people working on it.

        If 12 people take 3 hours to complete the harvest, how long will it take 9 people?

    ....

    (b) Find the time taken by 10 machines to make the same quantity of gears that 8 machines can make in 5 hours.

    ....

    (c) A ship has sufficient food to cater for 250 passengers for 6 days.

        (i) For how many days can it cater for 300 passengers? ....

        (ii) How many passengers can it cater for on a 15-day cruise?

        ....

Factorising Quadratics

1 Use expressions from the box to factorise the quadratics below.

| $2x + 3$ | $x - 5$ | $2x - 5$ | $x + 3$ | $2x + 5$ | $x + 5$ |

(a) $2x^2 - 7x - 15 = ($ ....$)($...$)$

(b) $4x^2 - 25 = ($ ....$)($...............................$)$

(c) $x^2 + 8x + 15 = ($ ....$)($.....................................$)$

2 **Solve** these quadratic equations by factorising:

(a) $x^2 + 9x + 20 = 0$ ....

....

(b) $3x^2 - 4x - 4 = 0$ ....

....

(c) $2x^2 + x - 28 = 0$ ....

....

(d) $m^2 - 4m = 0$ ....

....

3 Rearrange and solve these quadratic equations:

(a) $x^2 = 15 - 2x$ ....

....

(b) $4y + 5 = y^2$ ....

....

(c) $12 = 3x^2 - 5x$ ....

....

The Quadratic Formula

1 The 'quadratic formula' can be used to solve equations of the form $ax^2 + bx + c = 0$.
Write down the values of a, b and c in the equations below:

(a) $x^2 + 2x - 5 = 0$ $a =$ .... $b =$ .... $c =$ ....

(b) $2x^2 - 5x + 1 = 0$ $a =$ .... $b =$ .... $c =$ ....

(c) $5x^2 - 7x - 2 = 0$ $a =$ .... $b =$ .... $c =$ ....

2 The expression $b^2 - 4ac$ can be used to determine how many solutions a
quadratic equation $ax^2 + bx + c = 0$ has.

(a) Explain why there will be no solutions if $b^2 - 4ac < 0$.

....

....

(b) Determine whether the following quadratic equations have any solutions:

(i) $x^2 - 3x + 4 = 0$ ....

(ii) $2x^2 + 4x = 7$ ....

3 Solve these quadratic equations. Give your answers to 3 decimal places.

(a) $x^2 + 5x + 3 = 0$ ....

....

....

(b) $2x^2 - 7x = -2$ ....

....

....

(c) $3x^2 - 2x = 4$ ....

....

....

Completing the Square

1 Choose a bracket and a number from the box to complete the square for each quadratic equation below.

Brackets:	$(x + 5)$	$(x + 4)$	$(x + 3)$	$(x - 1)$
Numbers:	26	19	4	2

(a) $x^2 + 8x - 3 =$ ....$^2 -$ .... $= 0$

(b) $x^2 + 6x + 7 =$ ....$^2 -$ .... $= 0$

(c) $x^2 + 10x - 1 =$ ....$^2 -$ .... $= 0$

(d) $x^2 - 2x - 3 =$ ....$^2 -$ .... $= 0$

2  Express each of the following as a completed square:

(a) $x^2 - 6x - 4 = 0$ ....

....

(b) $2x^2 + 12x + 14 = 0$ ....

....

3 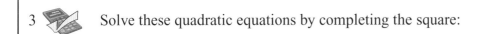 Solve these quadratic equations by completing the square:

(a) $x^2 + 4x - 5 = 0$ ....

....

....

(b) $x^2 - 3x = 3$ ....

....

....

(c) $3x^2 + 12x - 9 = 0$ ....

....

....

Simultaneous Equations

1 Follow the instructions to solve the sets of simultaneous equations:

    (a) $x^2 + y = 4$ and $y = 4x - 1$

        (i) Form a quadratic in x by substituting for y.

        ....

        (ii) Solve your quadratic equation to find two values of x.

        ....

        ....

        (iii) Find the corresponding values of y.

        ....

    (b) $x^2 + y = 2$ and $y = 4x + 5$

        (i) Form a quadratic in x by substituting for y:

        ....

        (ii) Solve your quadratic equation to find two values of x.

        ....

        ....

        (iii) Find the corresponding values of y.

        ....

2 Solve these pairs of simultaneous equations:

    (a) $x^2 + y = 6$ $2x + y = 3$

    ....

    ....

    ....

    (b) $3x^2 = y + 5$ $y - x = 2$ (Give your answers to 2 decimal places.)

    ....

    ....

    ....

Trial and Improvement

1   The equation $x^2(x + 1) = 56$ has a solution between $x = 3$ and $x = 4$, as shown below.

When $x = 3$, $x^2(x + 1) = 3^2(3 + 1) = 36$ (too small)

When $x = 4$, $x^2(x + 1) = 4^2(4 + 1) = 80$ (too big)

(a) Calculate the following:

$3.3^2(3.3 + 1) =$ ....

$3.4^2(3.4 + 1) =$ ....

$3.5^2(3.5 + 1) =$ ....

$3.6^2(3.6 + 1) =$ ....

$3.7^2(3.7 + 1) =$ ....

(b) Using your calculations from part (a), determine the solution of $x^2(x + 1) = 56$, correct to 1 decimal place.

....

2   Use trial and improvement to solve these problems to the degree of accuracy stated:

(a) The area of a rectangle is $h(h - 1) = 75$ cm^2, where h is between 9 cm and 10 cm. Find h correct to 1 decimal place.

....

....

....

....

....

(b) The equation $y = x^3 - 5$ crosses the x-axis between $x = 1$ and $x = 2$. In other words, the solution of $x^3 - 5 = 0$ is between 1 and 2. Find the value of x correct to 2 decimal places.

....

....

....

....

....

Compound Growth and Decay

1. If interest is added to an account at the end of each year, work out how many years it takes to double your money for each of the following rates of interest:

    (a) An interest rate of 5% per annum. ....

    ....

    (b) An interest rate of 9% per annum. ....

    ....

2. During the first hour of an 8-hour shift, a machine produces 480 bolts.

    (a) If the production rate drops by 10% every hour, how many bolts will be produced in the second hour?

    ....

    (b) How many bolts will be produced in the last hour of the shift?

    ....

    ....

3. Answer the following questions about exponential growth and decay:

    (a) The population of fish in a lake is estimated to decrease by 8% every year.
    How many will be left after 15 years if the initial population is 2000?

    ....

    ....

    (b) A new house cost £120 000, but increased in value by 15% each year.
    Work out its value after 5 years, to the nearest £1000.

    ....

    ....

    (c) The speed of a toy car running around a track falls by 10% every lap.
    If the speed on the first lap is 4 m/s, how fast will it be travelling on the sixth lap?

    ....

    ....

Variation

1 Complete these statements of proportionality. The first one has been done for you.

(a) $T = k\sqrt{W}$ T is ......*directly*...... proportional to ......*the square root of W*......

(b) $A = kh^3$ A is .... proportional to ....

(c) $y = \dfrac{k}{x^2}$ y is .... proportional to ....

(d) $M = \dfrac{k}{\sqrt{d}}$ M is .... proportional to ....

2 Choose the correct value of k for each statement below from the box.

| 1.5 | 18 | 2.4 | 10 |

(a) b is proportional to h^2, and when $b = 90$, $h = 3$. $k =$ ....

(b) f is proportional to v^3, and when $f = 12$, $v = 2$. $k =$ ....

(c) x varies with the square root of y, and when $x = 12$, $y = 25$. $k =$ ....

(d) p is inversely proportional to r^2, and when $p = 2$, $r = 3$. $k =$ ....

3 Round a bend on a railway track the height difference (h) between the outer and inner rails must vary in direct proportion to the square of the maximum permitted speed (S).

(a) If $h = 35$ mm when $S = 50$ km/h, write an equation relating h and S.

....

....

(b) Calculate h when $S = 40$.

....

....

4 The value of y is inversely proportional to the cube of x. Also, $x = 8$ when $y = 1.5$. Find the value of y when $x = 2$.

....

....

....

Algebra Mostly Mini-Exam (1)

1   This question is about solving equations by completing the square.

(a) Find the values of a and b such that:
$$x^2 - 6x + 4 = (x - a)^2 + b$$

....

....

(b) Hence or otherwise solve the following equation. Leave your answer in the form $p \pm \sqrt{q}$.
$$2x^2 - 12x + 8 = 0$$

....

....

2   This question is about factorising and simplifying expressions.

(a) Factorise completely:
(i) $2y^3 + 4y^2$

....

(ii) $y^2 - 4$

....

(b) Hence, simplify the expression $\dfrac{2y^3 + 4y^2}{y^2 - 4}$.

....

3   Solve the equation $4(p + 1) + 3(2p - 7) = 8$.

....

....

4   Solve the inequality $-3 < 2(x + 1) < 5$.

....

....

....

Algebra Mostly Mini-Exam (1)

5   This question is about factorising and solving quadratic equations.

    (a) Factorise the expression $2x^2 + x - 6$.

....

....

    (b) Hence solve the equation $2x^2 + x - 6 = 0$.

....

....

6   Solve the simultaneous equations:

$$x^2 + y = 6$$
$$7x = 3 + 2y$$

    Do **not** use a trial and improvement method.

....

....

....

....

7   D and H are both positive quantities. D is directly proportional to the square of H.
    When $D = 12$, $H = 4$.

    (a) Express D in terms of H.

....

....

    (b) Calculate D when $H = 8$.

....

....

    (c) Calculate H when $D = 3$.

....

....

Algebra Mostly Mini-Exam (2)

1 Solve the equation $\dfrac{2x+1}{5} + \dfrac{x+9}{3} = 1$.

....

....

....

2 Solve the inequality $\dfrac{2x+1}{5} + 3 < 0$.

....

....

3 Susie is using trial and improvement to find a solution to the equation $x^3 + 4x = 50$.
This table shows her first two tries:

x	$x^3 + 4x$	Comment
3	39	too small
4	80	too big

Continue the table to find a solution to the equation, correct to 2 decimal places.

Final answer: ....

4 Solve the quadratic equation $2x^2 - 3x - 7 = 0$.
Give your solution correct to 2 decimal places.

....

....

....

....

Algebra Mostly Mini-Exam (2)

5   Mr. Jones invests £5000 at an interest rate of 7% per annum.

(a) How much interest will he earn in the first year?

....

(b) Calculate the value of his savings after 5 years.

....

....

(c) How many years will it be before he doubles his money?

....

....

6   The quantity x is proportional to y^3.

(a) When $y = 5$, $x = 200$. Find the value of x when $y = 3$.

....

....

The quantity y is also inversely proportional to the square root of z.

(b) When $y = 10$, $z = 9$. Find the value of z when $y = 12$.

....

....

7   The triangle on the right has an area of 44 cm².

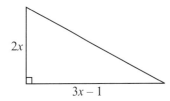

(a) Write an equation for the area in terms of x.

....

(b) Solve the equation to find the length of the shortest side of the triangle.

....

....

....